Church and Countryside

Church and Countryside

Insights from Rural Theology

Tim Gibson

scm press

© Tim Gibson 2010

Published in 2010 by SCM Press
Editorial office
13–17 Long Lane,
London, EC1A 9PN, UK

SCM Press is an imprint of Hymns Ancient and Modern Ltd
(a registered charity)
13A Hellesdon Park Road
Norwich NR6 5DR, UK
www.scm-canterburypress.co.uk

Scripture quotations are from the New Revised Standard Version
of the Bible, copyright 1989 by the Division of Christian Education
of the National Council of the Churches of Christ in the USA.
Used by permission. All rights reserved.

British Library Cataloguing in Publication data

A catalogue record for this book is available
from the British Library

978-0-334-04203-7

Originated by The Manila Typesetting Company
Printed and bound by
CPI Antony Rowe, Chippenham, SN14 6LH

Contents

Introduction

For me, this book has been about more than the production of a sustained argument concerning the interaction of the Church in the countryside with rural communities. It has involved reflection on a context that I have known intimately since childhood, and cared passionately about for just as long. It has been about locating my own practice in a theological method I have long admired.

Rural theology is not really a discipline. The literature with which I engage in the following pages comes from varied stock. There is good work being undertaken in the fields of rural mission and evangelism, and rural pastoral ministry. There is a large corpus of work concerned with the study of rural church attendance, and this has also helped in my research and writing. And, of course, there is the report produced by the Archbishops' Commission on Rural Areas, *Faith in the Countryside* (1990), which this year celebrates its twentieth anniversary. Of all the volumes on the rural context this is the one that has been most significant to my thinking.

Faith in the Countryside provides a basis for the theological reflection on the countryside in this book. That is not to suggest that I am offering a twenty-first-century update to the report: I did not have the resources to undertake such a project, and nor would I have wished to do so. But the document sets out the parameters of theological discussion concerning the countryside, and I am indebted to its authors.

As the references in these pages reveal, I am even more indebted to the theological method associated with the likes of Stanley Hauerwas and Samuel Wells. The insight of these thinkers is that what Christians do in worship makes a difference to their interaction with the world around them. At the heart of such an approach lies an appreciation of the Eucharist as the central formational practice of the Church, through participation in which we come to take our place in the drama of salvation history. This is a very particular way of viewing the world, and will not be to every reader's taste. For me, though, it is a way of thinking about rural life which enables us to connect our worship of the trinitarian God to our lives of love and service in the wider world.

Despite my enthusiasm for this way of doing theology, I have been surprised by the extent to which my reflection on the practical contributions church members might make to rural life bears it out. When I presented some of my thoughts to a local deanery chapter meeting, one of the attendees remarked that it was 'simple stuff'. He meant it as a compliment, I think, and I hope he was right in his assessment. What I offer in the following discussion ought to be simple, because a life of discipleship is straightforward. It involves acting on the basis of the habits we form through regular participation in the worshipping life of the Church.

To give an analogy: when one first learns to drive a car, one has to think about every separate element of the process in order to get it right: pulling off from a junction involves setting the gas, lifting the clutch to biting point, checking the rear-view mirror, twisting one's head to check the blind spot and – eventually – juddering away. More often than not, in the early days at any rate, the engine stalls and the whole process starts again. As time moves on, though, one becomes more adept at executing the various elements that make up the action of driving, and eventually they can be put together more or less by instinct. Driving becomes something that we can do out of habit, rather than a set of individual processes that have to be worked through each time we wish to move a car forwards or backwards.

A life of Christian discipleship is not dissimilar, in so far as it is something that we get better at doing through practice, and that can eventually become instinctual. Moreover, it is something in which we experience false starts, and in the doing of which even the most experienced practitioner will from time to time stall, or make mistakes. We learn how to be a Christian disciple who acts in Christlike ways through our participation in the practices of the Church, and most particularly through our eucharistic sharing of bread and drinking of wine. I argue in the following pages that the rural church is able to tell the best story about community, because a life of discipleship is concerned with imaging the trinitarian God, who is other-facing. The members of the rural church come to take this story for granted as a result of their participation in the Eucharist.

Christian disciples act in Christlike ways instinctually, because they have been formed to share Christ's love and justice with the world. Such an insight is the starting point for my reflections about the interaction of the Church in the countryside with rural communities. In Chapters 1–3, I attempt to explain why this theological basis is the best one available for thinking about rural life. The first three chapters constitute what I term a 'primer' in rural theology: an outline of its shape and methods, which inform the reflections in Chapters 4–7, concerning how Christians interact within their rural communities. This second half of the book is therefore where the insights gained from rural theology are brought to bear on rural life in the twenty-first century.

The practical ideas formed by these insights, and presented here, are intended as suggestions only. There are of course other ways in which Christians who live in the countryside contribute to their communities, and these will flow just as readily from the habits formed through their participation in the Eucharist. But I hope to show that they are simple, straightforward suggestions, in which Christians image the trinitarian God in profound ways. It might be said that the practical suggestions in this book are deceptively simple; or that their simplicity is a mark of their theological underpinnings.

In Chapter 1, I engage with the drama of salvation history by which Christians believe earthly life is constituted. I argue that a new creation is initiated through Christ's saving work, in which humans are called to a restored relationship with God. This means that they are called to a restored relationship with the rest of creation, and with one another, as those who image the trinitarian God and wait with eager longing for God's good future. This theological story is central to Christian self-understanding, and it informs a concern in rural theology for the nature of the relationships humans have with the non-human creation, and between themselves. Rural theology therefore has a particular focus on deepening relations between the species, and on resisting individualism.

In Chapter 2, I suggest that the Eucharist is a means by which Christian people discern what it means to live in community. I establish that the rural context in particular is fertile ground for this idea, since many rural and would-be rural dwellers are attracted to life in the countryside precisely because it promises stronger bonds of mutuality and reciprocity. That does not mean we can ignore the downside or, as I shall call it, the 'ugly underside' of community – its potential for oppression and creating feelings of isolation. But the eucharistic community is characterized by friendship, unselfishness and a willingness to forgive mistakes. It is also inherently focused on the life of the world. If such communities have an underside, we should have to say that their members are failing to image God.

Chapter 3 attempts to demonstrate why the theological story concerning rural community is the best one available. I argue that those who are formed through participation in the Eucharist contribute to the lives of their local communities, because they recognize that doing so is good, of itself. Attempts to describe the contributions of church members to rural life by reference to the positive consequences of their behaviour, or in terms of their contribution to the social capital of their communities, are impoverished. This is because they assume that people are compelled to engage in community life for reasons of personal gain, rather than because they recognize the intrinsic value of living in community with one's fellow creatures. Therefore, rural theology tells a different story from secular narratives concerning life in the countryside; we should resist the urge to dilute this story in order to express ourselves in terms designed to appeal to secular hearers.

Chapter 4 considers the proper role of rural theology when it comes to engaging with practical issues in rural life. It then offers an examination of the ways in which the Church's eucharistic life intersects with issues relating to food and farming. Chapter 5 engages in a similar activity, focused this time on rural services, and schools in particular, while Chapter 6 considers how humans interact with the rural landscape in their leisure time. In each of these chapters, my hope is to show how the insights gained from the theological approach outlined in Chapters 1–3 can guide the ways in which rural church members build community in their local areas.

Finally, in Chapter 7, I ask about the rural church's own life, and how its members can be most effective in sharing Christ's love and justice with the world. I explore the idea that, if participation in the Eucharist is central to Christian formation, the Church ought to find ways of reducing restrictions on who can receive Holy Communion, and the regularity with which the Eucharist can be celebrated in rural areas, where priests are in short supply. By adopting strategies that bring more members of its local community into its worshipping life, the rural church is better equipped to live its theological story in ways that share Christ's love and justice with the world.

I am grateful for the insights and criticisms of a variety of people with whom I have rehearsed my ideas, or who have read drafts of what appears in the following pages, and especially for the suggestions of the SCM readers who commented on an early proposal for the book and helped me to tighten its structure. I am also greatly indebted to Dr Natalie Watson, Senior Commissioning Editor at SCM Press, for her faith in this project.

Students and colleagues at the Southern Theological Education and Training Scheme (STETS) in Salisbury will be all too familiar with much of what is here, and I thank them for helping to sharpen my thinking over five years of fruitful and enjoyable work together. I also thank Professor David Catchpole for keeping me on the boil intellectually during countless shared car journeys. David has not read any of what follows, but he will doubtless recognize much of the content from what I have said as we career along the A303 together. I greatly prize his company on these journeys, and give thanks for the characteristically generous way in which he keeps an eye out for me, his former student.

Writing a book is at once the most enjoyable and the most infuriating thing in the world. I have been like a bear with a sore head in my parents' house and in my own, and I am grateful to Mum and Dad and my wife Sarah for putting up with it, and so much more, over the past year. For their part, Mum and Dad taught me when I was very young how the Church can help rural communities to flourish; their own rich ministry in the countryside echoes throughout these pages. And in addition to enduring countless dog walks in which I have expounded my latest Big Idea, Sarah helped with the painstaking task of tidying up my clumsy phrases, missed keystrokes and bad referencing. There is no way I can choose between these three people, who bring such sunshine into my life, and so I dedicate this volume, with profound gratitude, to all of them.

Tim Gibson,
Palm Sunday, 2010

1

The Hope of Rural Theology

This chapter provides a theological starting point for our reflections about life in the countryside. It seeks to identify the basic characteristics of the Christian story that we tell about God's creation, and our place within it. It makes the claim that theology is contextual, which is to say that it is lived in particular times and places, by and among particular people. It establishes two of the basic elements of rural theology, which have to do with recognizing the proper relation of humans to the rest of creation and to one another, and identifies the beginnings of a way in which Christians can live their story in community in rural surroundings.

A theological beginning

As humans made in the image of the Triune God we are called to be relational beings. Our fundamental orientation, like the Triune God, is to the other, whose existence we support and on whom we depend for our own existence. The Christian life is thus a life in which we hold the good of our fellow creatures as close to our hearts as we do our own – if not closer. It is a life that is oriented to helping other people, to helping them flourish in the hope that, by so doing, we live in communities of faith that are themselves a foretaste of Christ's kingdom.

In so far as this is the hope of all theology, rural or otherwise, it should seem an unsurprising place for us to begin. Few theologians would take issue with the idea that what it means to be human is bound up with what we term 'salvation history'. This is the drama of God's covenantal relationship with the created order, which has been marred by the fall and restored through the saving work of Christ. Because of our wilfulness, expressed in the story of the fall in Genesis 3, we humans have been estranged from God, and his image in us is marred. Thus, our existence becomes incomplete and we are in need of redemption. Such redemption comes through God's incarnation and death on a cross. It is achieved through the resurrection, which inaugurates a new creation in which we are called to live as those who are restored to a right relationship with God and with our fellow creatures.

This is the world in which we now live: a world from which the risen Christ has ascended, and in which we are striving for the coming kingdom in which God will be all in all. This is a world in which we seek to image the trinitarian God in profound ways, in ways that reflect our reconciliation to God through Christ, sustained by the Holy Spirit, and our hope for God's good future. As Christians, we are hopeful people and recognize that our orientation to God's future imposes certain expectations upon us. We are called to live as a restored community; we are obliged to live a life in which the good of the other is our primary concern. In short, we are a new creation. That is our place in the drama of Christian salvation history, as those who are reconciled to the trinitarian God whom we seek to image, and whom we worship on our knees.

So this is our starting place for rural theology. As I have said, it is uncontroversial in so far as it reflects the story the Christian community tells about itself. It is a story that we repeat in our liturgies in church and in our private devotions. It is the story that defines us as those who are called to be members of Christ's body here on earth. If somebody were to ask you what it means to be Christian, this is the story with which you might answer.

2

Theology is alive and life-giving

As we are constantly reminded, it is a characteristic of this story of salvation history to be rooted in particular contexts. Inasmuch as it constitutes not only our foundational narrative but also the basis of our Christian doctrines, we cannot but remember its origins in particular historical circumstances. The stories we read in the Bible – individual chapters which come together in the service of the overarching narrative of which Scripture speaks – are stories about a particular set of people, rooted in particular times and places. They are stories of Israelites and Egyptians, Jews and Greeks. They are stories of patriarchs and kings, of husbands and wives. They are stories of rich and poor, of men and women, of apostles and unbelievers. And, perhaps more fundamentally, they are stories about us – you and me – because they tell us who we are.

Similarly, Christian doctrine, which provides us with a set of beliefs by which we are constituted, is inherently bound to particular contexts. The creeds are by no means fixed abstract statements of faith (although we might sometimes treat them as if they are, not least when we recite them in stilted tones while facing east on a Sunday morning). At their best, the creeds are capable of receiving expression in ways that bring life to the circumstances with which we are faced, as are the doctrines to which they refer. As a now somewhat old-fashioned handbook to the Apostles' Creed reminds us: 'The mystery of the Trinity must still be understood as a living and life-giving reality, and not just as a theoretical framework, a convenient catalogue of the essential truths of our faith.'[1]

In similar vein, Daniel Migliore states, 'Christian theology arises out of, and remains importantly linked to, a particular

---

1 Bezancon, Jean-Noel, Ferlay, Philippe and Onfray, Jean-Marie, 1987, *How to Understand the Creed*, London: SCM Press, p. 7.

community of faith.'[2] This means that Christian doctrine is alive, as Christ is alive, in a range of contexts. Wherever we are as God's creatures, we are called to give joyful expression to our faith. Whatever circumstances we are confronted by, we respond in ways that embody our fundamental beliefs, and those beliefs adjust, advance and alter in the face of our lives with one another. Christian theology is not fixed or static: it is a vibrant, living and exciting activity in which all of us who profess faith in Christ are caught up.

It is helpful here to think of Mike Higton's analogy of theology being like the performance of a piece of music. For Higton, theology is about embodying Christ's love and justice in particular ways, in particular places and with particular people. Higton avers that theology is about living a godly life, and says that the performance of our place in the Christian story that I have described above is akin to the performance of a piece of music. Although we learn general things about the performance – the place of the notes in the piece, say, its rhythms and dynamics – each performance is an individual event, because 'all those generalities become subservient to the particular occasion, shaped by particular circumstances in ways that are unrepeatable'.[3]

So our performance of our place in the Christian story of salvation history is necessarily contextual. The story, like a piece of music, has generic features, of course. Its notation, if you will, is centred on the trinitarian God, its rhythm is structured in ways that allow us to image that God, and its content is the good news of creation's covenantal relation to him. But when we perform it in the precise circumstances with which we are faced on a day-by-day basis, we do so in ways that are necessarily context-specific. Or, to put it another way, our theology is both universal,

2 Migliore, Daniel, 1991, *Faith Seeking Understanding: An Introduction to Christian Theology*, Grand Rapids: Eerdmans, p. xii.

3 Higton, Mike, 2008, *SCM Core Text: Christian Doctrine*, London: SCM Press, p. 47.

because it speaks of the God who is creator of the whole universe, and particular, because it involves becoming like the Christ who was incarnate at a particular time and in a particular place.[4]

So the fact that this book is concerned with *rural* theology rather than any other type is important. The precise landscape – physical and social – of the rural context will colour any attempt to reflect theologically on issues relating to life in the countryside. But more fundamentally, I want to argue that rural theology is about embodying our beliefs about who we are as Christians in ways that give life to the rural communities of which we are a part. There is thus a twofold process behind rural theology: on the one hand, what we think we know of God is likely to be influenced in profound ways by our location in particular rural contexts. On the other hand, how we live in the rural contexts in which we are located is coloured by our commitment to Christian salvation history. Neither can be separated from the other; Christian rural theology is alive and life-giving, because it speaks of the Christ who is alive and who gives life to the world.

The new creation

If God has ordered a new creation through the life, death, resurrection and ascension of his son Jesus Christ, then we already live in a new order. The fallen world has been reconciled to God, and as those who are called to a restored relationship with the Triune God, humans must respond appropriately. But what does such a response entail, and how is it shaped in particular by the experience of living in a rural environment?

That is one of the questions posed by the Church of England's report about rural affairs, *Faith in the Countryside* (1990). The report was produced by the Archbishops' Commission on Rural

---

4 Sobrino, Jon, 1978, *Christology at the Crossroads: A Latin American Approach*, London: SCM Press, p. 388.

Areas, and contains a detailed and helpful analysis of many of the issues relating to rural life towards the end of the twentieth century. Many such issues remain important, as the second half of this book demonstrates, and the report precipitated a renewed interest in theological engagement with life in the countryside among church members, and by the Church at institutional level. One of the most significant fruits of *Faith in the Countryside* was the appointment of a National Rural Officer for the Church of England, whose job is centred on facilitating and providing a lead on the interaction of theology with rural life, and vice versa.

Reflecting the idea that theology arises out of particular contexts just as much as it is lived in particular contexts, the report contains a theological reflection on rural life fairly early in its pages (chapter 2). The authors observe that this reflection emerged as much from the Commission's ongoing research as it did colour the members' interaction with rural issues. So the twofold nature of rural theology is enshrined in the work of the Commission, with theology informing and being informed by its participants' reflections on rural life.

At the heart of the theological reflection in *Faith in the Countryside* is a concern to discover a 'context of reference concerning what human beings and nature are, and what they may both become in the light of the overall purposes of God'.[5] For the report's authors, therefore, the question of the nature of humanity in the new creation inaugurated by Christ's saving work is fundamental to the task of rural theology.

I would like to divide my beginning of a response to this question into two parts: first, I shall consider the idea that, in rural theology, humans must have a right relationship with the rest of creation; and second, I shall consider the idea that rural theology requires

---

5 Archbishops' Commission on Rural Areas (ACORA), 1990, *Faith in the Countryside*, Worthing: Churchman Publishing, p. 8, using a quotation from Arthur Peacocke, 1979, *Creation and the World of Science*, Oxford: Oxford University Press.

humans to have a right relationship with one another. Both of these ideas are central to my approach, and one cannot be identified as more important than the other. They are, if you like, the test of rural theology. But more than that, they constitute its essential character and provide two generalities which we are called to perform in particular ways, depending upon our circumstances.

Human beings and the rest of creation

In 1967, Lynn White Junior delivered a damning indictment of Christian theology. In a paper entitled 'The Historical Roots of our Ecologic Crisis', he argued that Christianity encourages an attitude of dominance by humans in relation to the natural world. White's critique centres on the creation narratives of Genesis 1, and he summarizes their content thus:

> Finally, God had created Adam and, as an afterthought, Eve to keep man from being lonely. Man named all the animals, thus establishing his dominance over them. God planned all of this explicitly for man's benefit and rule: no item in the physical creation had any purpose save to serve man's purposes. And, although man's body is made of clay, he is not simply part of nature: he is made in God's image.[6]

White argues that the attitudes contained in the Genesis account of creation helped shape an ongoing disposition by humans toward the natural environment that consistently places human interests above those of the rest of the created order. This is the sense of his term 'anthropocentric', which means, quite literally, 'human-centred'. The assumption that White believes to be so damaging in

---

6 White Jr, Lynn, 1967, 'The Historical Roots of our Ecologic Crisis', available in Robin Gill (ed.), 2006, *A Textbook of Christian Ethics*, Edinburgh: T&T Clark, p. 307.

Christian discourse is the idea that humans, made in God's image and foreshadowing the form of the incarnate Christ, share God's transcendence over nature and can therefore use it to their own ends, without reference to what is good for the non-human world.

The assumption that White accuses the Christian narrative of making concerning the relation of humanity to the non-human world is in need of correction. To put it another way, there is something profoundly untheological about an assumption of human supremacy over the rest of creation. It is untheological precisely because it assumes that we are somehow elevated over the other creatures, as if God has singled us out for an individual fate. It assumes, that is to say, that the hope of theology is a uniquely human hope, and this is to misappropriate the creation narratives in ways that take us away from our call to be Christlike. In other words, the assumption that humanity has dominance over the non-human world is a fallen assumption: anthropocentrism is a sign of our fallen state, and needs to be redeemed.

Let us consider Karl Barth's summary of the doctrine of creation. Barth states:

> Creation comes first in the series of works of the Triune God, and is thus the beginning of all the things distinct from God himself. But, according to the biblical witness, the purpose and therefore the meaning of creation is to make possible the history of God's covenant with human beings, which has its beginning, its centre and its culmination in Jesus Christ. The history of this covenant is as much the goal of creation as creation itself is the beginning of this history.[7]

At first sight, this might be taken to reinforce just that anthropocentric world-view that White condemns. Barth states that 'the

---

7 Barth, Karl, 1958, *Church Dogmatics III: The Doctrine of Creation, Pt I*, Edinburgh: T&T Clark, p. 41.

purpose and meaning of creation is to make possible the history of God's covenant with human beings', which might be taken to presuppose that God's interaction with the created order is primarily centred on humankind, as if the rest of the world is there only as a stage on which the drama of salvation history can be played out.

This reading of Barth's summary of the doctrine of creation, however, fails to set it within the wider context of the drama of salvation history. For, as Colossians 1.13–23 reminds us, creation is not merely the backdrop for humanity's covenantal relation with God. Rather, creation is an aspect of God's covenantal relationship with all that is, human and non-human. It is a *part of the story*. According to Barth, God creates in order to save: when you put it like this, any assumption that the story of salvation history is a uniquely human story seems bizarre. When God creates the world, he intends to reconcile the whole of creation to himself through Christ. Humans have a particular role in this process of reconciliation, because they share in the redemptive project as those who image the Triune God. But that does not entitle humans to plunder the earth, or to prioritize our own interests over those of the non-human creation, because all of God's creatures are equal in sharing in the narrative of salvation.

The reason our imaging of God does not entitle humans to dominate the rest of the created order is because the world is part of God's providential purposes, rather than merely being the context in which those purposes are worked out. Orthodox Christian belief, as Colin Gunton reminds us, holds that the 'whole creation, and particularly the sinful human creation, is in need of redemption by a God who is other than it because, as it is, it fails to achieve its proper end'.[8] Thus, creation in its entirety is

---

8 Gunton, Colin, 1997, 'The Doctrine of Creation', in Colin E. Gunton (ed.), *The Cambridge Companion to Christian Doctrine*, Cambridge: Cambridge University Press, p. 155.

fallen, and caught up in God's redemptive work through Christ. It is not only humans who will be saved, but the rest of the world as well. For this reason, the hope of Christian theology is a hope for the whole of creation; to elevate humans above the natural world is to forget that the world itself is part of the drama of salvation history.

Besides, rural life in particular reminds us of our dependence on God's created order. As Gunton remarks, 'A garden without a gardener will produce little of the food and other necessities for the life of the one who is, furless and clawless, among the most vulnerable of the world's species.'[9] Recognizing this, we can begin to come to terms with our dependence on the non-human world, which argues against an irresponsible attitude towards it. Our role is God-given, and we are made in his image. But imaging God means that we have a particular concern for the flourishing of the rest of creation – something that we are constantly reminded of by our dependence on it for existence. Our flourishing is intimately tied to the flourishing of the creation. That is not in itself a good enough reason to take particular care of the natural world. But if we suppose for a moment that God makes us dependent upon the world around us in order to keep us humble, and that our failure to remember such dependence is one of the ways in which God's image in us is marred, then it becomes plain that Christian theology is not inherently anthropocentric – or that, in any case, it ought not to be.

Thus, White's recommendation that Christians might begin to pay particular attention to the spirituality of St Francis of Assisi can be helpful. St Francis was committed to the idea of the equality of all God's creatures, calling every animal a brother or sister in Christ.[10] Such spirituality might seem like so much New Age dross to contemporary ears, but it reminds us of the need to treat

---

9 Gunton, 1997, 'The Doctrine of Creation', p. 155.
10 White, 1967, 'The Historical Roots of our Ecologic Crisis', p. 310.

every aspect of creation with appropriate respect. It reminds us of the need to have a right relationship with the rest of creation.

Faith in the Countryside calls for a reinterpretation of a Christian theology of creation in ways that acknowledge the idea that redemption has to do with the integrity of the entire world, and is not focused only on humans. The idea is hardly new, as we see when we remember St Paul's comments in his letter to the Romans:

> For the creation waits with eager longing for the revealing of the children of God; for the creation was subjected to futility, not of its own will but by the will of the one who subjected it, in hope that the creation itself will be set free from its bondage to decay and will obtain the freedom of the glory of the children of God. We know that the whole creation has been groaning in labour pains until now . . . (Romans 8.19–22)

As the authors of Faith in the Countryside note, the idea that humans are related to the non-human world and that salvation history concerns the universe as a whole rather than being a uniquely human story has always been implicit in Christian theology.[11] The current ecological changes taking place in the world are a stark reminder of this fact, and remind us also that the assumption that human interests are to be prioritized over non-human interests is a sign of our failure to image the trinitarian God, who creates and sustains the universe.

Similarly, the report's authors acknowledge the interdependence between the human and the non-human world. They acknowledge the reliance of humans on the world for food and shelter, and they identify a distinctive role for humans as those who are able to serve as representatives of the non-human world. 'The non-human world of animals, plants and inorganic matter

---

11 ACORA, Faith in the Countryside, p. 10.

cannot represent its own interests', says the report. 'This world needs a voice and a champion, now as never before.'[12] It is my contention that unless humans provide such a voice, unless we are champions of the natural world and recognize its intrinsic value, we fail to image the trinitarian God. That, it seems to me, is a more appropriate way of understanding our God-given role in relation to the created order than the idea that we should dominate the non-human world and use it to our own ends. That is the basis on which we resist White's charge of anthropocentrism, and can be certain of having a right relationship with the rest of creation.

Human beings and one another

So much for the relation of humans to the non-human world. If we are to attend to this aspect of rural theology, we also need to attend to our relationships with one another. Unless we are able to take the interests and concerns of our fellow human beings seriously, then it is unlikely we will be able to enter into a right relationship with the rest of creation. After all, as the above analysis reminds us, we seem to have a predisposition to accord more weight to human interests than to anything else. That is to say, if we fail to look after one another, then we are unlikely to take appropriate care of the world around us. And, putting the two things together, we will be unable to image God, who is Trinity, and perform our part in the story of Christian salvation history.

The authors of *Faith in the Countryside* recognize the importance of human beings having a right relationship with one another. They identify the pervasive individualism embodied in Margaret Thatcher's infamous denouncement of the idea of society as posing a serious problem in rural life, and representing

---

12 ACORA, *Faith in the Countryside*, p. 15.

a threat to rural theology in particular.[13] If there is no such thing as society, as Mrs Thatcher is claimed to have said, but only collections of individuals, then the idea of a community of faith that is called to embody the Christian story in particular rural contexts will struggle to get off the ground.

Individualism poses a serious problem for rural theology. It tells a story that is conceptually incommensurate with the Christian narrative of becoming Christlike, and embodying his love and justice. Individualism is out of step with a commitment to image a trinitarian God, whose fundamental nature is other-facing. An individualistic society will not be one where notions of community have much currency, nor where people are persuaded of the intrinsic worth of coming together with others to worship God and give thanks and praise for all that he has done. Quite apart from encouraging a prioritizing of human interests over non-human interests, individualism encourages a prioritizing of *my* interests over *yours*. It undermines the hope of rural theology because it conceives the person as a single unit, rather than as a relational being who participates in his or her own way in the economy of God's saving work. To put it differently, it reinforces a fallen idea of human beings as isolated, self-interested and detached from the other creatures.

Faith in the Countryside is not alone in assuming that the eighteenth-century Enlightenment played a significant role in replacing ideas of human mutuality and interdependence with an understanding of the person as a self-in-isolation.[14] The philosopher Alasdair MacIntyre has traced this argument in a persuasive fashion, most clearly in a book entitled *After Virtue*. MacIntyre argues that the Enlightenment emphasis on rationality, the exercise of reason in discerning what one ought to do and on the nature of existence, led human beings

---

13 ACORA, *Faith in the Countryside*, p. 18.
14 ACORA, *Faith in the Countryside*, p. 19.

to become disconnected from the contexts in which they lived. The idea that being human consisted in abstract rational reflection thereby became enshrined in western culture, such that the concept of personhood became associated with nothing more than the individualized exercise of reason. Human beings were no longer constituted by and through their relationships with one another, therefore, but by their ability to think rationally about the world in which they lived.[15] Human persons came to be viewed as free-floating individuals, primarily defined by their cerebral activity, rather than as embodied persons-in-community whose fates are intrinsically linked with one another and with the rest of the world.

Whatever its origins, we see individualism given clear expression in those attempts to order society in ways that try to mitigate the negative effects of self-interest. The two things appear to go together, since if I am concerned primarily with my own good, it stands to reason that I will pay little heed to the interests of anyone other than myself. So we see, for example, in John Rawls's influential theory of justice an attempt to ameliorate the impact of a very human vice: the desire to preserve one's own interests over and above those of other people.

Rawls imagines a world in which individual human beings agree to participate in society only on grounds that it is the best way of preserving their own interests so far as possible. The other option for self-interested people – namely anarchy, an absence of societal order – is not worth risking because although it promises absolute freedom to pursue one's own ends without intervention, it is likely to cause more harm than good. In a world without order, where humans are self-interested and individualistic, the Hobbesian image of a war of all against all becomes an inevitable reality. I might be free to look after number

---

15 MacIntyre, Alasdair, 1985, *After Virtue: A Study in Moral Theory*, London: Duckworth.

one, but if everyone else does the same then it is unlikely any of us will prosper.

The Rawlsian approach is an example of 'social contractarianism'; its assumption is that human agents are willing to participate in society in order to preserve their own interests. Society only exists as a means of keeping rampant self-interest in check, and the idea of community is more or less redundant. Rawls imagines that human beings will go behind a 'veil of ignorance' in order to settle upon the rules by which their society is to be governed. Behind this veil, we have no knowledge of our position in life, of our wealth or our status: each person is equal in the sense that we do not know who is at the top of the social ladder and who is at the bottom. Because of this, Rawls identifies the risk that any one person behind the veil of ignorance could be among society's worst off – but, of course, they do not know it. To compensate for this, Rawls believes that self-interested humans behind the veil of ignorance will settle on rules that are most advantageous for those at the very bottom of society, on grounds that, just in case that is where they land up, they will not suffer too much hardship.[16]

Rawls's approach bears closer scrutiny because it yields a society that appears on face value to embody many features that Christians would associate with the new creation inaugurated by Christ's life, death, resurrection and ascension. Rawls's approach leads to equality, fairness and a particular concern for those at the very bottom of society. But these values are not motivated by other-regard, as they are in the Christian story which identifies imaging the trinitarian God as central to the performance of our part in salvation history. Rather, they are motivated by a concern to look after ourselves; Rawls assumes that the only way to enshrine these egalitarian features in a society of self-interested

---

16 Rawls, John, 1971, *A Theory of Justice*, Cambridge, MA: Harvard University Press.

individuals is to provide a mechanism by which we choose them for our own sake, rather than for the good of other people. The approach tells a very different story from the Christian one of salvation history on which I have focused in this chapter, because it is underpinned by the assumption of individualism and, with it, self-interest. We might say that Rawls's conception of personhood is fairly pessimistic, therefore. He assumes that we cannot be trained out of the individualism and self-interest that as Christians we would want to say are part of our fallen state, and that society needs to be ordered in ways that ameliorate the negative effects of our fallen natures. My attempt to map the beginnings of an approach to rural theology in this book resists individualism, and seeks to tell a more optimistic story about personhood that views humans as inherently relational and called to live in restored community as part of their imaging of the trinitarian God in the new creation.

Social contractarianism has an echo in the idea of social capital, which I critique in Chapter 3. In both cases, the assumptions made about what it is to be human – what theologians mean by the term 'anthropology'[17] – seem far removed from the theological story of humanity as being made in the image of the trinitarian God whose fundamental nature is oriented to the other. Even when a philosophical position, such as that of Rawls, yields a society that bears hallmarks of the kingdom, as it were, we will want to tell an alternative story that resists individualism and identifies other-regard as a characteristic of redeemed human nature.

Set alongside the concern of rural theology to ensure that human beings have a right relationship with the rest of creation is this concern, that humans have a right relationship with one another. This means that rural theology resists individualism

17 Banner, Michael, 2006, 'A Doctrine of Human Being', in Michael Banner and Alan Torrance (eds), *The Doctrine of God and Theological Ethics*, Edinburgh: T&T Clark, p. 139.

and emphasizes the role of community in human life, as *Faith in the Countryside* rightly identifies.[18] Rural theology emphasizes the role of community not because it hankers after some idealized, and probably unhistorical, understanding of rural life taken from the pages of Miss Marple stories and the books of James Herriot.[19] Rather, it emphasizes the role of community because to do so is to make a commitment that is profoundly theological, a commitment that encourages the Church in the countryside to respond to God's call to live in his image, and inspires rural church members to play their part in the drama of salvation history as those who are reconciled to God in a new creation.

A theological story about rural life

Reflecting theologically about the contemporary rural context provides an exciting opportunity to explore notions of community. The members of the Archbishops' Commission on Rural Areas interacted with many vibrant communities during the course of their research,[20] and it is clear even two decades later that many rural dwellers have not abandoned the idea of community entirely. Indeed, for many people choosing to move into the countryside, the promise of a communal life marked by mutuality and interdependency is a considerable draw, as I explore in the next chapter.

This might seem promising, given the concerns I have outlined already in this chapter, and that pervade the rest of this book. But I argue that using the language of community is insufficient in itself unless it is underpinned by a deep retelling of the story of what it is to be a human being made in God's image, whose fundamental

---

18 ACORA, *Faith in the Countryside*, p. 18.

19 Smith, Alan, 2008, *God-Shaped Mission*, Norwich: Canterbury Press, p. 3.

20 ACORA, *Faith in the Countryside*, p. 18.

character is to face the other. The idea of rural community is too often held up without serious thought as a solution to the problems affecting the countryside and its inhabitants, but it has been insufficiently worked out, and therefore lacks an explanatory narrative. Or worse, it is, like Rawls's theory of justice, underpinned by individualistic and anthropocentric assumptions, rather than a serious commitment to the relational nature of humanity. Such a commitment is found in the Christian story of salvation history which I have begun to unpack in this chapter, and which comes alive in the Eucharist. It is a story that speaks of humans as being inherently relational, living for one another and for God, rather than for themselves. It is a story that requires of humans that they are in right relationship with the rest of creation, which is also bound up in God's saving work, and that they are in right relationship with one another. When such requirements are met, participation in community is not reduced to a means of ameliorating the effects of self-interested individualism. Rather, participation in community is part of our fundamental character as human agents who are called to image God who is Trinity. It is part of our participation in the new creation inaugurated by Christ's saving action. It is part of what it means to be human.

2

Exploring Community

This chapter is concerned with unpacking the idea of community introduced at the end of Chapter 1. In exploring the idea of rural community in more detail, I begin by uncovering the ways in which the rural context provides a particular opportunity for thinking about community in relation to ethics. Rural areas are associated with having strong community links, and many contemporary rural and would-be rural dwellers continue to be impressed by the idea of living in a close-knit community. Such communities are not necessarily positive, however, as a brief examination of their ugly underside illustrates. Moreover, an attempt to make notions of community central to ethical discourse lays one open to the charge of romanticism. In resisting this charge, I would say that community is not merely a good idea for Christian ethicists with an interest in rural affairs: it is part of who we are as God's people. In other words, Christians are called to live in community and to share the goods of communal living with the rest of the world. Christian theology tells us why community is a characteristic of the new creation. The eucharistic practice of the Christian community encourages its members to take the right things for granted, and therefore to serve the world around them. Finally, I offer a rebuttal of the idea that emphasis on Christian community as a basis for rural theology might lead the Church to become segregated, or to withdraw from the world. As it happens, a church community whose common life is centred on the Eucharist cannot but be fully engaged with the world it is called to serve.

The rural idyll

Rural theologians are understandably wary of reinforcing stereo-typical images of rural life. It is common to see them following the lead of *Faith in the Countryside* by dismissing the idea of the rural idyll as 'myth'.[1] And it is true that what many regard as the traditional image of the British countryside is rather outmoded, and may never have existed in many places. But whether it was a historical reality or not, the rural idyll continues to exert a considerable pull over rural and would-be rural dwellers, and is at least part of the reason why so many people wish to move to rural areas from towns and cities. The Commission for Rural Communities' *State of the Countryside* report identifies consid-erable internal migration from urban and suburban areas to ru-ral settlements – a pattern the report's authors attribute to the 'perceived better quality of life' in the countryside.[2] A key fea-ture of this perceived improvement in the quality of life among rural dwellers is the greater levels of reciprocity and commu-nity involvement that are expected among people living in the countryside, as a report by the Countryside Agency (the former name of the Commission for Rural Communities) recognized in 1999. The report, *Living in the Countryside: The Needs and Aspirations of Rural Populations*, states: 'The perceived strength of the community is one of the most prized features of rural life – an asset that is largely seen to be lost in urban areas.'[3] The ap-peal of the rural idyll, such as it is, explains why the government

---

1 ACORA, 1990, *Faith in the Countryside*, Worthing: Churchman Publish-ing, p. 1; see also Smith, Alan, 2008, *God-Shaped Mission*, Norwich: Canter-bury Press, p. 3.

2 Commission for Rural Communities (CRC), 2008, *State of the Country-side*, p. 17.

3 Countryside Agency, 1999, *Living in the Countryside: The Needs and Aspirations of Rural Populations*, p. 24.

expects the rural population to have increased by 16 per cent by 2028.[4]

Whatever the truth behind the notion that rural life is characterized by close-knit communities whose members enjoy greater reciprocity than their urban counterparts, it continues to influence attitudes towards life in the countryside. This represents an opportunity for those, like me, who want to put the idea of community at the centre of thinking about rural life in the coming years, because it demonstrates that there is a commitment to the idea among those whose lives are centred on rural areas. So rather than simply dismiss the rural idyll as the stuff of fantasy, we should look more seriously at its appeal among rural dwellers, because this might provide a useful starting point for our reflections about life in the countryside.

I do not intend to romanticize rural life, or to paint a picture of a lifestyle that can never be realized in the contemporary world. But it is insightful to consider the origins of the view that life in the countryside can be community-centred, and to explore more fully what that might mean for the way in which we approach the activity of rural theology.

A trip to the country

While we might well be wary of reinforcing the idea that the rural idyll is only true in the pages of novels and on television screens, there is some merit in considering for a moment the literary presentation of rural life that appears to inform at least elements of contemporary thinking about it. Consider a brief snapshot from the parish magazine archives of the Wiltshire town of Wilton, taken from 1883. We are given an image of a husband and wife –

---

4 Taylor, Matthew, 2008, *Living Working Countryside: The Taylor Review of Rural Economy and Affordable Housing*, London: Department for Communities and Local Government, p. 8.

Mr and Mrs John Brooks – taking a walk out with one another after supper and encountering their neighbour – Mrs Harris – on the steps of her home. A conversation between the three parties reveals their shared life together: Mrs Harris asks how Mr Brooks is after his last bout of 'rheumatics' and they discuss the content of the Vicar's recent sermon on the subject of receiving Holy Communion. The episode reaches a conclusion with Mrs Harris inviting the Brookses in for a drink in her lounge.[5]

This incident embodies the image of rural life that I am arguing continues to exert a pull on rural dwellers today. There is a clear model of rural community at work in this episode, and it is close to the stereotypical image that many associate with life in the countryside: people who take walks after supper in order to enjoy the beauty of God's creation; who stop and talk with their neighbours and, in so doing, evince an easy familiarity and genuine engagement with one another's lives; who come and go from each other's houses and whose lives are very much focused on the activities of the local parish church. It is hard to imagine an example of the rural idyll which could contain any more of its classic components than this brief excerpt manages to. And while we might not wish to make a strong claim for the historical veracity of the incident described in the parish magazine, we can at least identify its influence on contemporary attitudes to rural life. When rural commentators talk about the quest by rural inhabitants for 'community and a more socially involved lifestyle,'[6] we must recognize that the quest is informed in no small part by images of rural life such as this one. Fact or fantasy, the rural idyll continues to inform our thinking about life in the countryside.

There is surely no better story told about a rural community than Ronald Blythe's oral history of a tiny composite village in

---

5 Clarke, J. Erskine (ed.), 1883, *Parish Magazine*, p. 9 of May edn.
6 Countryside Agency, 2002, *Rural Services Survey*, quoted in NCVO, 2003, *It's Who You Know: Social Capital in Rural Areas*, p. 2.

Suffolk, *Akenfield*, first published in 1967. Blythe's unique book has provided a foundational narrative for the ways in which we think about the countryside and its people, and it is doubly interesting because, like the parish magazine archives, it occupies a murky niche between fiction and social history. Whatever we make of its accuracy as a historical record, *Akenfield* provides an indispensable account of rural life in the mid twentieth century.

Blythe sought to capture the essence of his community by recounting conversations with three generations of residents: the elderly farmers and labourers who were born at the end of the Victorian period; their children, born in the years between the two world wars; and the 1960s' teenagers, discovering free love and on the cusp of the sort of individualistic, consumerist world-view that proliferates today, and that I discussed in the previous chapter. It is because of Blythe's skilful capturing of these three constituencies that his book stands out: his characters keep us in touch with the nineteenth-century world of the Brookses and Mrs Harris, but they are also looking towards the world we inhabit now, and wondering how things will turn out for rural communities in coming years.

There is nothing sentimental about Blythe's characterization of the countryside; he does not seek to defend the rural idyll. That aside, he describes a world of intimate connections across generations, where villagers know not only of their own origins, but of the other figures in the community and their role in its life. So, for example, the 44-year-old blacksmith Gregory Gladwell talks of his similarity to his grandfather, of his family's shifting political views over generations and how they have played out in village life, and of his likeness to a man of some fame in the community, Charles Bradlaugh. Gladwell's staff consists of local boys – born and educated in the village, and arriving with him straight from school to learn their trade.[7] His story is echoed in the lives of other characters across the pages of *Akenfield*.

---

7 Blythe, Ronald, 2005, *Akenfield*, London: Penguin Classics, pp. 109–18.

Blythe's unique skill lies in locating his insights about rural life in the lives of real people like Gladwell; giving authentic voice to their concerns, hopes and fears. Rather than dealing in the observation of general trends, or with dry statistics, Blythe provides a way of thinking about rural life that is grounded in the concrete experiences of real people. Blythe's very method is, in a sense, an embodiment of the insight I am expounding in this volume: that people matter, that communities matter, and that when we talk about the countryside we rightly focus on them.

Unsurprisingly, Blythe's approach is much imitated, and in no more direct a fashion than Craig Taylor's *Return to Akenfield*, in which the village is revisited, and the accounts of new interlocutors recorded. Like Blythe himself, Taylor captures the essence of the place and its people with striking economy, and his section about 'Incomers' is especially illuminating.[8] Of all the people who talk about the community of Akenfield, the new arrivals seem to care most deeply about it. They lament the fact that everyone travels by car, thereby removing the chance of bumping into one another in the village. They are actively involved with the church or the amateur dramatics society, and they despair at the lack of a decent village pub. Taylor's message is plain: the incomers have come in search of a particular way of life, and are disappointed to discover that it is not to be found – not, at least, in the measure in which they hoped to experience it.

The *Akenfield* literature provides a lyrical account of the point I am making: namely, that regardless of the historical veracity of what I am terming the rural idyll, it continues to exert a pull on rural and would-be rural dwellers. It plays a foundational role in how we think about life in the countryside. Because of this, I suggest that the rural context is one in which a rural theology that

---

8 Taylor, Craig, 2006, *Return to Akenfield*, London: Granta Books, pp. 37–53.

takes community to be a central motif is rooted in fertile ground. People, whether accurately or not, equate the countryside with strong bonds of community. For many, such bonds are a reason for living in rural areas. When it comes to encouraging people to live in ways that embody communal values, rural dwellers will not need too much persuasion.

Idealism and community

As Stanley Hauerwas reminds us, however, an attempt to make the concept of community central to ethical reflection and practice leaves one open to the charge of idealism. More fundamentally, he says, it leaves one vulnerable to the criticism that the 'ugly underside' of rural communities passes unrecognized, obscured as it is by cosier images such as I have been concerned with above.[9] The way to resist this charge is surely to show that one's conception of community is realistic and life-giving, as I hope to do in the second part of this book. But a good start to a response to this challenge is to acknowledge the underside of close-knit communities, if only in order to identify ways in which our own communities need to be different.

Blythe and Taylor recognized divisions among residents of Akenfield in their respective accounts of its common life. Tension between locals and incomers, conflict about the appropriate way to make use of the land, and rising house prices, all contribute to the melee in which both narratives are set. But in neither case is there so clear an example of the downside of close-knit rural communities as Thomas Hardy provides in *The Mayor of Casterbridge*. In the same way that the Wilton parish magazine archives and the *Akenfield* literature occupy a grey area between history and fiction, so too might we assume that Hardy's account

9 Hauerwas, Stanley, 1995, 'What Could it Mean for the Church to be Christ's Body?', *Scottish Journal of Theology* 48, p. 11.

of the narrow-mindedness of rural dwellers represents a merging of experience with creative licence. Hardy experienced the ugly underside of rural communities for himself when he was ignominiously forced to return to Bockhampton after failing to achieve literary fame during his five-year stay in London. Having left with grand ambitions, he received no small amount of derision at the hands of the villagers to whom he returned – his pretension to be different from them having led him to be treated with suspicion.[10]

Yet Hardy's own trials seem as nothing compared to the treatment to which he would subject his eponymous protagonist in *The Mayor of Casterbridge*. Michael Henchard, the disgraced former mayor, is discovered to have engaged in an affair with the wife of the current mayor, Donald Farfrae. As was customary in rural areas in England during the nineteenth century, and even witnessed as recently as the 1960s in East Sussex, Henchard and his lover are made the subjects of a 'skimmity ride'. This practice – also known as 'loo-belling' and 'riding the stang' – involved parading inhabitants of towns and villages thought to have been guilty of fornication or adultery in effigy around the area, with their neighbours shouting, screaming and banging drums while following behind. The idea was public humiliation of people whose conduct was thought to be immoral, and its effects must have been unimaginably horrid for the humiliated couple. In Hardy's account, Henchard's lover dies as a result of the shock of the episode, and he himself is left contemplating suicide.

Hardy no doubt emphasizes the horror of the skimmity ride for dramatic effect, but it serves as a striking image of what I am calling the 'ugly underside' of close-knit communities. Less dramatic, but nonetheless salutary, is the common experience of incomers to villages, who feel excluded by the strong bonds

---

10 Tomalin, Claire, 2006, *Thomas Hardy: The Time-Torn Man*, London: Viking, p. 87.

existing between long-term residents.[11] It is definitely the case even today that residents of rural areas tend to be fairly conservative in their outlook, and diversity is less common in the countryside than it is in towns and cities. This can lead some to feel excluded, or even oppressed, by the wider community with whose views their own seem to be out of step. Such feelings of exclusion are especially pronounced among young rural inhabitants, which might go some way to explaining why the 15–29 age group is the only one in which there is net migration away from rural areas.[12]

The point is plain, and simply made: when seeking to tell a positive story about community, such as I am trying to do in this book, it is important to remain aware of the underside of communities, which is evidenced in fiction and in fact. Even though the idea of community exerts a pull on rural and would-be rural dwellers, and the rural context is thus fertile ground for a theology in which community is central, the ugly underside of communities cannot be ignored. It is a reality for many people that their communities fail them: if rural theology is to make a difference to life in the countryside, the communities built by those who seek to image the trinitarian God and become Christlike need to be especially mindful of those who may be excluded or exist on the margins.

Theology and community

The theological story I am trying to expound concerning community has two features: first, it assumes that living in community is a part of our imaging of the God who is Trinity, and, second,

11 Davies, John S., 2004, 'Ethnicity and Diversity', in Jeremy Martineau, Leslie Francis and Peter Francis (eds), *Changing Rural Life*, Norwich: Canterbury Press, p. 181.

12 CRC, *State of the Countryside*, p. 18.

it argues that such imaging involves forming communities in which Christ's love and justice are known by everyone, from which nobody is excluded. The first feature has already been evidenced in the discussion in Chapter 1, in which I established the other-facing character of human existence in the new creation, while the second feature arises partly in response to recognition of the underside of community. It is, of course, unreasonable to suppose that Christian communities consisting of members who embody their part in the drama of salvation history should be in any way perfect. As Tim Gorringe reminds us, we are apprentices who 'bodge things and make countless mistakes'.[13] We are in the process of learning what it means to live as people of the kingdom, existing as we do in the in-between times of God's saving work. We are resurrected people, but we are not fully redeemed, or else Christ's saving work would be done. Our part in salvation history is as those who hopefully await our full redemption by joining creation's groaning, and waiting with eager longing for God's good future. If as humans we are called to image the trinitarian God through our right relationship with creation and with one another, we are also aware that we will fall short and fail from time to time. That is our place in the scheme of salvation; it is what defines our humanity.

Even so, we are encouraged to try to image the trinitarian God, because we know that it is our task as human beings to do so. Difficult as it may be, we are sustained in our lives of Christian discipleship through the practices that define us as a people. These practices are our opportunity to recount the narrative of salvation history that helps us to remember who we are. Foremost among them is the Eucharist, which has a central and important role in the kind of theology I am outlining. Following Stanley Hauerwas and Sam Wells, I want to say that 'through worship God trains

---

13 Gorringe, Timothy, 1997, *The Sign of Love: Reflections on the Eucharist*, London: SPCK, p. 29.

his people to take the right things for granted'.[14] In the Eucharist, God gives his people everything they need to embody their place in the drama of salvation, to become his companions and to be formed in his image.[15] As Timothy Radcliffe has pointed out, the Eucharist provides a structure through which we recall the story that makes us who we are, through which we share in God's life and come to be defined as a people of hope:

> Each act [of the Eucharist] prepares for the next. By listening to the word of God, we grow in faith and so become ready to proclaim the Creed and ask for what we need. In the second act, belief leads to hope. From the preparation of the gifts to the end of the Eucharistic prayer, we remember how on the night before he died, Jesus took bread, blessed it and gave it to the disciples saying, 'This is my body, given for you.' Faced with failure, violence and death, we are given hope, repeating Christ's own prayer. In the final act, from the 'Our Father' onwards, our hope culminates in love. We prepare for Communion. We encounter the risen Christ and his victory over death and hatred, and receive the bread of life. Finally we are sent on our way – 'Go and serve the Lord' – as a sign of God's love for the world.[16]

Radcliffe's summary of the eucharistic structure bears detailed repetition because of its elegant capturing of the foundational character of the practice. In this account of the Eucharist, we see its role in forming God's people for the life to which we are called by virtue of Christ's saving work. The story of the Eucharist is the story of salvation history, which I have said defines us as Christian

---

14 Hauerwas, Stanley and Wells, Samuel, 2006, 'The Gift of the Church and the Gifts God Gives It', in Hauerwas and Wells (eds), *The Blackwell Companion to Christian Ethics*, Oxford: Blackwell, p. 25.

15 Cf. Wells, Samuel, 2006, *God's Companions*, Oxford: Blackwell.

16 Radcliffe, Timothy, 2008, *Why Go to Church?*, London: Continuum, p. 7.

disciples. Our regular participation in the feast transforms us as those who live that story for the good of the world, as signs of God's love for all creation. Thus Louis-Marie Chauvet states: '. . . faith is nothing other than the daily realization of what is lived in the symbolic experience of the Eucharistic meal: we must eat, masticate to the point of accepting, in heart and body, the bitter scandal of a God crucified for the life of the world'.[17]

When we come together as a community gathered around the eucharistic table, we are remembering our shared fate with one another and with the rest of creation. Therefore, we cannot but be reminded of the need for right relationship with the non-human and human world around us, since in the Eucharist we are brought into God's presence alongside our fellow creatures and drawn up into the drama and hope of redemption. This happens not least because, in sharing the eucharistic meal, we are sharing in the practice that Christ instituted with his disciples as a sign of their continued life in the kingdom, sustained by the Holy Spirit and waiting in anticipation of his return. Thus Paul, in the first letter to the Corinthians, states:

For I received from the Lord what I also handed on to you, that the Lord Jesus on the night when he was betrayed took a loaf of bread, and when he had given thanks, he broke it and said, 'This is my body that is for you. Do this in remembrance of me.' In the same way he took the cup also, after supper, saying 'This is the cup of the new covenant in my blood. Do this, as often as you drink it, in remembrance of me.' For as often as you eat this bread and drink the cup, you proclaim the Lord's death until he comes. (1 Cor. 11.23–26)

17 Chauvet, Louis-Marie, 1997, *The Sacraments*, Minnesota: The Liturgical Press, p. 50.

The Eucharist is God's gift to us, that we might be a gift to the world in which we celebrate it. The Eucharist is a reminder that we are called to face the other, as the trinitarian God faces the other in its fundamental nature, and that our lives of discipleship are rightly marked by our relation to our fellow creatures.

We can say more, and probably should, about the role of the Eucharist in forming us as Christ's disciples who are called to image the trinitarian God. At the very least, we can say the following three things: first, that the Eucharist shows us how to be friends; second, that the Eucharist trains us out of selfish ways; and, third, that, through the Eucharist, God forgives our mistakes.

The Eucharist shows us how to be friends

When Jesus knew he was to be betrayed, he shared supper with his friends. In that moment of high drama, Christ gathered around him those whom he loved, and ate with them (Mark 14.22–25; Matt. 26.26–29; Luke 22.15–20). Therefore, the Eucharist reminds us of Christ's friendship, or, as Wells and Hauerwas put it, it offers a model of human companionship with God and one another.[18] Gorringe is also persuaded of the significance of the Eucharist in forming people for friendship with one another. He believes that it can and must be a means of welcoming people to the Christian community of fellowship, since as a practice it gets to the heart of the Christian narrative:

> The situation of being 'in Adam', which did not end in AD 35 or thereabouts, but describes an ongoing human situation, is that of relationships of domination, hierarchy, division and the attempt to solve problems through law and violence. The situation of being 'in Christ' is that situation where there is 'no

18 Hauerwas and Wells, 'The Gift of the Church', p. 13.

Jew or Greek, slave or free, male or female' – where, in other words, our status as friends under God is recognized.[19]

Coming together in celebration of the Eucharist involves opening ourselves to life in Christ, therefore, which Paul describes in the quotation to which Gorringe refers in Galatians 3.28: 'There is no longer Jew or Greek, there is no longer slave or free, there is no longer male or female; for all of you are one in Christ Jesus.' The Eucharist, because it is that practice through which we are caught up in the drama of Christian salvation history and come to be formed in ways that make us Christlike, is a practice through which we are made friends with God and with one another, as brothers and sisters in the new creation. The eucharistic community is a friendly community; not in a glib way of offering tea and biscuits to newcomers (although this is never to be discouraged), but in a deep-rooted way that gets to the heart of what it means to be human. Unless those who eat Christ's body and drink his blood are inherently centred on the good of the other, as Christ was in his eucharistic offering, then they cannot be said to image God. To put it another way, the Eucharist transforms us to become members of a community in which we recognize our common humanity in Christ, and stand before him as those who await his coming in glory as one body, sustained by his Spirit.

The Eucharist trains us out of selfish ways

If we are shown how to be friends through participation in the Eucharist, we are also trained out of selfishness in order to serve the good of the other. Selfishness clearly has no place in the kingdom inaugurated by Christ's life, death, resurrection and ascension, since the other-facing character of those called to image

---

19 Gorringe, *Sign of Love*, pp. 30–1.

God cannot be reconciled to the pursuit of one's own goods at the cost of another. In other words, selfishness is a trait of the old – fallen – order, while other-regard is a sign of the kingdom, made real in the sharing of Christ's body and blood.

When put this way, the feeding of the multitude, which is recounted in each of the four Gospels, might have a very different explanation from the miraculous multiplication of bread and fish that conventional biblical interpretation has assumed. It is worth noting that the episode has clear eucharistic overtones, particularly in the Johannine account. The fact that it is followed by the 'bread of life' discourses of John 6.22ff. seems to reinforce the idea that the fourth evangelist believed himself to be describing Christ's institution of a practice that was to be central in Christian life. Note how in John 6.11 we see Jesus taking the loaves and giving thanks over them before distributing them among his followers. The words echo those that we associate with the Last Supper – an episode that does not appear in the expected place in John's Gospel (that is, prior to Christ's arrest). Thus, the feeding of the multitude might well be expected to tell us something about the Eucharist, especially the version of it that appears in John's Gospel.

Even if the traditional interpretation is accepted without question, the fact that this story might be associated with the Church's eucharistic practice is important. It reminds us of God's abundant gifts to the world he has created, such that even in times of shortage he provides his creatures with an excess of his good gifts. But an alternative reading, such as the one recounted by Gorringe, might tell us even more about what it means to be a human participant in the Eucharist, attempting to image God and being formed through regular sharing of his body and blood.

Gorringe wonders whether the feeding of the multitude is less a story about Christ's miraculous production of abundant food from scarce resources, and more about Christ's miraculous overcoming of human selfishness through the breaking and sharing of bread. Noting that it is a child who comes forward to offer his food to the crowd in the Johannine account (John 6.9), Gorringe states:

> It seems much more beautiful, and much more in keeping with the Jesus who refused signs to prove his messiahship, and resisted the temptation to turn stones into bread, to believe that the boy's artless willingness to share shamed others into sharing what they also brought with them.[20]

Compared to the story told about human co-operation in John Rawls's theory of justice, which I explored in the previous chapter and in which an attempt is made to ameliorate the negative effects of self-interest in order to produce a just society, this story is more compelling, and offers more hope to a world in which poverty is the experience of many. According to Gorringe, the feeding of the multitude – a story that is eucharistic in tone – is concerned with retraining human desires so that they work for the good of other people, rather than for the good of self. Every time we participate in the Eucharist, we are reminded not only of Christ's self-giving in his crucifixion, but perhaps also of the significance of sharing between humans in the new creation. The Eucharist is thus the practice through participation in which we are formed to have a right relationship with one another, because it educates our desires away from selfishness and towards the good of the other. It is the practice through participation in which we come to image the trinitarian God, to share in Christ's love and justice, to become like that person who consistently reminded us to share and to look out for one another. Whether we find Gorringe's reinterpretation of the feeding of the multitude persuasive or not, the Eucharist is clearly centred on sharing and mutuality, and the community that celebrates it attempts to tell a story about human nature that

---

20 Gorringe, *Sign of Love*, pp. 33–4.

resists selfishness. Such a community becomes counter-cultural, therefore, in so far as it believes humans can be trained out of selfish ways; that common life is about the good of the other, rather than the good of oneself.

Through the Eucharist, God forgives our mistakes

If John 6 carries what I am terming 'eucharistic overtones', then the same is certainly true of the Gospel's final chapter. In John 21, the risen Christ appears to his disciples, who are disconsolate and lacking in purpose since his death on the cross. No disciple is in a worse state of mind than Simon Peter, who is wracked with guilt over his denial of Jesus prior to his crucifixion (John 18.15ff.; Luke 22.54ff.; Mark 14.66ff.; Matt. 26.69ff.). But the risen Christ offers Peter his forgiveness, in a conversation that mirrors the threefold pattern of Peter's denial. As Timothy Radcliffe notes, John's recounting of the incident is especially telling, since the situation beside a charcoal fire exactly replicates Peter's location when his faith faltered (John 18.18).[21] Let us remind ourselves of the detail of Jesus' exchange with Peter:

> When they had finished breakfast, Jesus said to Simon Peter, 'Simon, son of John, do you love me more than these?' He said to him, 'Yes, Lord; you know that I love you.' Jesus said to him, 'Feed my lambs.' A second time he said to him, 'Simon, son of John, do you love me?' He said to him, 'Yes, Lord, you know that I love you.' Jesus said to him, 'Tend my sheep.' He said to him the third time, 'Simon, son of John, do you love me?' Peter felt hurt because he said to him the third time, 'Do you love me?' And he said to him, 'Lord, you know everything; you know that I love you.' Jesus said to him, 'Feed my sheep. Very

---

21 Radcliffe, *Why Go to Church?*, p. 192.

truly I tell you, when you were younger, you used to fasten your own belt and to go wherever you wished. But when you grow old, you will stretch out your hands, and someone else will fasten a belt around you and take you where you do not wish to go.' (He said this to indicate the kind of death by which he would glorify God.) After this he said to him, 'Follow me.' (John 21.15–19)

What this episode shows is Jesus' infinite love for his creatures, through which he accepts our frailties and failures and gives us space to be what we cannot help but be – namely fallen creatures in need of redemption. In this incident, as Radcliffe says, Peter comes home to Jesus.[22] And since this gathering of the disciples with the risen Christ to share a meal with him is a harbinger of the Eucharist we celebrate Sunday by Sunday in our churches, it reminds us that we find our home in Jesus through the sharing of this resurrection meal. We come to the table in all our weakness, and yet we are transformed by the saving power of God's love for his creatures. The eucharistic community is by no means a perfect one, therefore, but it is one in which we are loved because of our imperfections. And, because of this, all are welcome at the table, to share in Christ's body and blood and take their place in the drama of salvation history.

A rural retreat?

In emphasizing the significance of the Eucharist in the formation of a community through which we can engage with rural life, I am inevitably making the Church central to theological engagement with rural life. In other words, by suggesting that rural theology is about the participation of Christian disciples in the Eucharist,

---

22 Radcliffe, *Why Go to Church?*, p. 194.

through which they come to take the right things for granted, I might be accused of an undue narrowing of focus, on those who belong to the Church; I might be seen to be advocating a retreat of the rural church away from the wider community. But, I suggest, to make such an accusation is to misunderstand the fundamental character of the Eucharist. For by its nature the Eucharist intersects with the world in which it is celebrated. It is a worldly practice in which bread is given to the hungry (as in John 6) and through which the whole creation – not just the part that goes to church – is transformed.

Thus, the Eucharist is for the good of the world, rather than the good of those who participate in it. When I say that the Eucharist is the means by which we are formed to take our part in the drama of Christian salvation history, I am saying that the Eucharist is the means by which we come to embody those dispositions that enable us to share God's gifts with the rest of the world. Or, to put it another way, the Christian community celebrates the Eucharist in order to be a Eucharist for the world, thereby coming to share Christ's love and justice far and wide. Rather than being a practice that is exclusive and constitutive of a narrowly defined membership, therefore, the Eucharist is a means by which we can do rural theology in ways that make a tangible difference to the wider communities of which we are a part. Precisely because the idea of community that I am expounding here is intimately linked to the regular celebration of the Eucharist, it generates a theology that is engaged, looks outward to the world beyond the churchyard and encourages all to participate in the new creation promised by Christ's redemptive work. It reconciles the whole of creation to God, not just the Church.

Of course, on a very practical level, participation in the Eucharist can be seen to make a difference to how people think about ethical issues facing them in day-to-day life. In her book about Christian ethics and work, Esther Reed introduces the idea of 'liturgical reasoning'. As a concept, it bears no easy explanation, but it has to do with the way in which ideas can crystallize, and clarity can be arrived at, through and during participation in an act of worship. It might be compared to the experience one has when trying to see a particular star or constellation in the night sky. Sometimes, by looking slightly away from where we think the star is, it jumps into focus on the periphery of our vision. Liturgical reasoning is similar: we are engaged in an act of worship – let us say the Eucharist – when suddenly we realize how best to deal with a particular situation or problem that is in the back of our mind. Reed provides an example: 'I sang the hymn "My song is love unknown" recently. It caused me somehow to think of an elderly lady for whom this hymn was a great favourite, and spurred me into writing her a letter the next day.'[23]

Whatever is going on here, it is certain that the activity of worshipping God helps participants to achieve some clarity in their decisions, and it might even be guiding their actions. What is more, it seems likely that the values to which the hymns they sing and the liturgies they recite bear witness will have an impact on their attitudes and opinions. To put it another way, not only will Christians be able to think more clearly about issues and concerns when they are worshipping God, but their response to these issues and concerns will be informed by their participation in the worshipping life of the Church.

The latter point is explored in detail by Robin Gill in his study of the impact of churchgoing on congregation members.[24] After extensive engagement with the responses of Christians in surveys such as the British Household Panel Survey, Gill concludes that churchgoing makes a noticeable difference to the ways in which people typically respond to ethical dilemmas. Regular participation in worship forms disciples in distinctive ways, as those who

---

23 Reed, Esther, 2010, *Work, For God's Sake*, London: Darton, Longman and Todd, p. 37.

24 Gill, Robin, 1999, *Churchgoing and Christian Ethics*, Cambridge: Cambridge University Press.

are called to play their part in the drama of salvation history. Moreover, liturgical reasoning suggests that people might well be able to reach clarity about particular issues more readily when they are engaged in an act of worship, such as the Eucharist.

The practice of the Eucharist shapes us to respond to the world around us in distinctive ways. When we exercise liturgical reason, we come to conclusions about life in the presence of God the creator. It should come as little surprise, therefore, that we achieve greater clarity when in the presence of the trinitarian God in worship, and that our focus goes beyond the narrow concerns of the worshipping community. God is creator of all that is, human and non-human. If coming into his presence through participation in the eucharistic life of the Church forms us and enables us to think more clearly about particular problems or concerns, it would be more surprising if it did so only in relation to the life of the Church.

More fundamentally, though, the accusation I have imagined, that the approach to rural theology I am outlining in this book could be taken to advocate a retreat of the rural church away from the wider community, cannot be made if we understand the Eucharist properly. As Tim Gorringe states, the description of the Eucharist as 'the Mass' comes from the Latin version of the dismissal: '*Ite, missa est*', 'Go, it is the dismissal'. This reminds us that the Eucharist is 'not introverted, a wallow in religious sentiment, but extroverted; that Christians only gather in order to better perform their task "in the world"'.[25] The Eucharist finds its denouement in the moment at which those who have participated in it, who have shared body and blood as part of the new creation reconciled to God through Christ, are sent out into the world to share God's gifts with it.

To assume that a eucharistic rural theology is anything other than focused on the life of the community in which the Church

25 Gorringe, *Sign of Love*, p. 67.

in the countryside is set is to forget that the Eucharist finds its raison d'être in the closing sentences of its liturgy. In the Anglican celebration, we are told at the end to 'Go in peace to love and serve the Lord'. It is this life of service, the sharing of God's gifts with the rest of creation, which lies at the heart of the approach I am taking in this book. As Timothy Radcliffe states in answer to his own question: 'Why go to church? To be sent from it.'[26]

26 Radcliffe, *Why Go to Church?*, p. 208.

3

Having Faith in Rural Theology

I argue that, through the Eucharist, the rural church is formed as a community that shares Christ's love and justice with the world around it. In other words, the rural church can be a Eucharist for the communities in which it is set, and in which it is called to love and serve the Lord. In this chapter, I want to explore what that might mean. Churchgoers make a significant contribution to community life in rural areas. I want to make sure that the story we tell about such a contribution is properly theological. To that end, I shall explore the limitations of secular understandings of community that accord the concept only instrumental worth, on the basis of the benefits that accrue to people as a result of participation in community life. Community has intrinsic worth, because living in community is part of our imaging of the trinitarian God, who is himself communal. This is the theological story of community, derived as it is from the narrative of salvation history that I have written about in previous chapters. The Eucharist is the Church's way of embodying that narrative, and living as community in ways that show the world what it means to live for one another, as Christ lived and died for us. Finally, therefore, I urge that we have faith in rural theology as telling a distinctive story about community. This does not preclude engagement with secular narratives about rural life, but keeps us mindful of the distinctive contribution the Church can make to it. To put it another way, because the Church tells the best story about community, we must be careful that its contribution to rural life is not diluted by a desire to express ourselves in terms that are acceptable to secular discourse.

Churchgoing and rural community

In 2006, researchers working on behalf of the Arthur Rank Centre in Stoneleigh, Warwickshire, published the results of an extensive project in which they sought to identify the contribution of churchgoers to life in rural communities. The subsequent report, *Faith in Rural Communities*, provides empirical support for what many suspect anyway: namely that 'people who attend church regularly make a significant contribution to community vibrancy'.[1] The report notes that churchgoers are more likely than non-churchgoers to engage in activities such as caring for the elderly, visiting the sick and undertaking voluntary childcare.[2] Moreover, it observes that such people are also more likely to participate in other community clubs and associations, such as Parent–Teacher Associations, the Women's Institute and local Age Concern groups.[3] The researchers also indicate that churchgoers are more likely than non-churchgoers to participate in activities in the wider voluntary sector, such as National Park committees, sports clubs and the Round Table.[4] These three types of activity might be characterized in three ways, which will be helpful in subsequent discussion: (1) engaging in the life of the local community; (2) being involved in different groups and networks within the community; and (3) being involved in groups and networks outside the community.

---

1 Farrell, Richard, Hopkinson, Jill, Jarvis, David, Martineau, Jeremy and Ricketts Hein, Jane, 2006, *Faith in Rural Communities*, Stoneleigh: ACORA Publishing, pp. 6–7.

2 Farrell *et al.*, *Faith in Rural Communities*, p. 28.

3 Farrell *et al.*, *Faith in Rural Communities*, p. 32.

4 Farrell *et al.*, *Faith in Rural Communities*, p. 39.

However they are categorized, the activities described in the report are all examples of a higher engagement in rural community life among churchgoers in comparison to their fellow rural dwellers, who are not involved in the worshipping life of the Church. This is obviously encouraging so far as my argument in this volume is concerned, since it suggests the truth of my assertion that churchgoing *makes a difference*. When worshippers are dismissed from the Eucharist, they appear to take seriously their responsibility to love and serve the Lord, by sharing God's gifts far and wide. Such an assumption is given support by the findings reported in *Faith in Rural Communities* concerning the motivation of churchgoers for their higher than average level of community engagement. The researchers found that respondents to their surveys spoke of six broad types of motivation:

- involvement in community life flows from life as a person of faith – that is, regular prayer and worship provides a basis for right living;
- involvement in community life is a 'practical and visible outworking of faith';
- involvement in the community falls to churchgoers because no one else is willing to do it;
- it is the Church's role (and therefore its members' responsibility) to 'makes things happen' in the community;
- involvement in community life is 'just part of life'; and
- a blending of the previous five types of motivation.[5]

In each of these cases, the motivation appears to stem from recognition that participation in the life of the wider community is good in itself. None of the respondents suggested that their motivation stems from a sense in which they contribute to the community because of what they can get out of it for themselves.

5 Farrell *et al.*, *Faith in Rural Communities*, pp. 44–5.

Rather, their motivations talk of what we might call a sense of duty or obligation to help others; a duty or obligation that stems from their participation in prayer and worship, or from an understanding of their faith, or their view of the wider role of the Church in community life. Even more encouragingly, some respondents cannot delineate their motivation; saying that involvement in the life of their community is just what they do, or something that they take for granted.

Rather like Robin Gill's research that I mentioned in the previous chapter, about the impact of churchgoing on the attitudes of congregation members,[6] the findings of this research indicate that regular participation in the Church's worshipping life appears to make a difference to how people live and act in their communities. The kinds of activities that the *Faith in Rural Communities* report describes as typical of regular church attenders are activities that flow naturally from participation in the Eucharist, through which I am arguing we are shown how to be friends and trained out of selfish ways. When people who undertake such activities in their communities are asked about their motivations, they seem to be saying that they act in such a way because of their faith in, and worship of, the trinitarian God. The theological story of community that we tell about these findings is rich and deep; it is a story about what it means to take seriously our lives in the new creation inaugurated by Christ's life, death, resurrection and ascension.

It is for this reason, because of the richness and depth of the theological story concerning community, that I urge confidence in our telling of it. It is tempting, after all, for those of us who belong to the Church to express our story in different, unfamiliar language, in the hope that by doing so we will broaden its appeal to secular hearers. We feel driven towards this because so

---

6 Gill, Robin, 1999, *Churchgoing and Christian Ethics*, Cambridge: Cambridge: University Press.

much of the good work being undertaken by our brothers and sisters in Christ in the service of rural communities appears to be 'overlooked and undervalued' by the government and other interested parties.[7] The Church, in other words, does not appear to receive the recognition that we think it deserves in response to its contribution to rural life. And, in an effort to argue our corner, as it were, we adopt the language of secular discourses in order to express the Church's contribution in terms that our interlocutors in government and elsewhere will understand. I contend, however, that when we do this we run the risk of diluting the distinctive character of the rural church, which I am saying is grounded in the eucharistic life of its members. We risk selling out to secular mores in an effort to achieve recognition of our good works. And perversely, in so doing, we weaken the distinctive contribution that we as Christian disciples can make to life in the countryside.

So I am urging that Christians have faith in rural theology; in the telling of a theological story about rural life that places community at its heart and believes the Eucharist to be a central practice in the forming of God's people to serve the world. I am urging that we hold our nerve in saying that, when members of the Church contribute in profound ways to the life of their local communities, they are doing so because they wish to share Christ's love and justice among their fellow creatures. I am urging that when we talk about rural life, we do so in ways that are properly theological, rather than in ways that are designed to appeal to secular hearers. Because, when we do this, we are being true to our story, we are living our part in the drama of salvation history, and we will, I think, be taken more seriously as agents of transformation in the lives of our communities.

---

7 Langrish, Michael, 2006, 'Seeds in Holy Ground – A Future for the Rural Church? A Background Briefing from the Mission and Public Affairs Council', Warwick: ARC, pp. 1, 8.

Resisting temptation

Part of the problem, it seems to me, is the temptation presented by secular discourses that appear to talk about community in terms we find acceptable. When we identify a secular telling of the story of community that seems to fit our own, it is tempting to re-express our theological story in its terms. It is tempting to think that in this way we will show secular hearers that we are not so different, after all. And yet we are different, because we have a story to tell about community that is capable of 'out-narrating' the secular versions.[8] This is because the theological story of community recognizes it as good of itself, and does not express the value of community involvement by reference to the good things that flow for its members. In other words, the theological story ascribes intrinsic, rather than instrumental, worth to rural communities.

This might seem like a rather abstract and theoretical point, so allow me to examine it in the first instance by reference to a concrete example. There is a woman in my village whom I shall call Margaret. She is a retired schoolteacher, married and in her early sixties, whose children have left home and whose husband remains in full-time employment. Margaret is a weekly attender at the parish church; she sings in the choir, helps make the coffee after services, sits on the PCC and does her fair share on the church's cleaning rota. In addition to her various roles in the life of the church, Margaret is a governor of the village primary school, a member of the local quilting society and vice-chairwoman of the local Scout group. When she is not tied up with all these activities, Margaret helps her elderly neighbour Milly by collecting her newspaper and milk each morning from the village shop and making sure she has plenty of food in her store cupboards.

---

8 Shortt, Rupert, 2005, *God's Advocates*, London: Darton, Longman and Todd, p. 173 (Shortt is reporting a conversation with Stanley Hauerwas and Sam Wells).

Margaret feeds Milly at least twice a week, by sharing leftovers with her. She also takes a group of three elderly people into the local supermarket each week to stock up on groceries, and frequently goes to visit her friends in surrounding villages for coffee and lunch.

Like many of the respondents in the *Faith in Rural Communities* research, Margaret regards all of these activities as part of the life of service to which she is called through her membership of the Church. She might not think too explicitly about her motivations on a day-by-day basis, but she is clear about one thing: when it comes to helping other people and contributing to her community, Margaret does not do so because she thinks there is anything in it for her. Indeed, she would most likely be rather insulted if someone were to suggest the idea to her, since she regards many of the people with whom she interacts in the course of her various activities as her friends. Margaret helps other people and takes an active role in the life of her community because she recognizes it as a good thing to be doing. She is not hoping to be rewarded for her trouble, and she does not crave recognition. She merely wants to help.

Margaret will be a familiar figure to many of us. There are Margarets throughout the country, and all of them make a unique and wonderful contribution to the world around them. Their lives are truly eucharistic, in so far as they live the good news of the new creation for the good of the world. They are inspiring, and their example is salutary. It is for this reason that we must resist the temptation to retell the story of Margaret in ways that fail to do justice to her motivations for acting.

A 'consequentialist' account of community

One way in which we could offer such a retelling would be to provide what I shall term a 'consequentialist' account of Margaret's participation in the life of her community. Consequentialism is a term most readily associated with ethical theory, and it describes approaches to ethics that express notions of right and wrong by reference to the consequences of our actions. If an action produces the best possible consequences, it is regarded in such a schema as being right or good; similarly, if it produces the worst possible consequences, it is regarded as wrong or bad.

As an example of consequentialist analysis of human conduct, let us consider the moral question of whether one ought to break the speed limit or not. A consequentialist might reason that a person who is late for an appointment and is tempted to break the speed limit ought not to do so, on the basis that they could conceivably end up losing control of their vehicle and causing an accident, which is likely to cause harm to them and to other people. By reference to the consequences of the action, therefore, it is assessed to be morally wrong.

Imagine now, though, that the driver has a friend in the back who has cut his leg while using a chainsaw in his garden, and who appears to be losing vast quantities of blood. Time is very much of the essence, and the driver might well break the speed limit in order to get his friend to hospital as soon as possible. Given the likely consequences of failing to get the injured man to hospital quickly, a consequentialist may reason not merely that breaking the speed limit is acceptable in the circumstances, but that it is the *right* thing to do.

This simple example illustrates a key feature of consequentialist reasoning: it only ascribes value to human conduct by reference to its consequences. In other words, for the consequentialist, human actions are value-neutral; value can only be expressed by reference to the consequences of a particular act. Now, for the Christian ethicist, such an approach might seem to be out of step with the ways in which we standardly reach our conclusions about appropriate behaviour. To return to the speeding example, a Christian might well want to say that we ought never to break speed limits, because doing so embodies a recklessness concerning creaturely life which is out of step with our belief that we need to be in right relationship with one another and with the rest of creation. That is not to say that the Christian would not countenance the breaking of a speed limit in order to rush an injured friend to hospital (in such circumstances, we might say, in contrast to the consequentialist, that the principle of not breaking speed limits can be put on hold, because it is overridden by the more pressing need to relieve our friend's distress – but that is another matter). It is, rather, to acknowledge that the story we tell about our conduct is different, because it ascribes value to our actions independently of the consequences which may or may not result from them.

A consequentialist retelling of Margaret's engagement with the life of her community would be unjustly reductionist. It would reduce our assessment of it (and therefore make an assumption concerning Margaret's own assessment of it) to the positive consequences that ensue from her actions. So we would say that Margaret's contribution to her community is good because it benefits a variety of people – most obviously Milly and the weekly supermarket shoppers, but also the Scouts, the quilters, the school pupils, and so on. We might also say that Margaret's contribution to her community is good because the strong bonds of friendship and support that her activities engender make the village a nicer place in which to live. And we might, finally, suggest that Margaret's contribution to her community is good for Margaret, because it makes her feel good to help other people and to have friends, and because it increases the chances of people helping her if ever she should need it.

But to tell Margaret's story in this way is to ignore what her actions reveal about the love of a trinitarian God who would invite us to become his friends in the Eucharist, and give us everything we need to take our place in the drama of salvation history. It would obscure the Christlike character of Margaret's conduct, as one whose vocation is to share Christ's love and justice with the world. By reducing our assessment of Margaret's activities in her community to an assessment of the consequences of her various actions, we fail to attend to their intrinsic worth as acts of faithful discipleship; we ignore Margaret's obedience to God and what he reveals of himself through her, and in the Eucharist.

The churchgoers whose opinions were canvassed in the research for *Faith in Rural Communities*, like Margaret, believe that their actions show something of the Christ who lives and dies for the world, whose Spirit sustains us in a new creation in which we wait with eager longing for our promised future. They might not express their motivations in such richly theological language, but they reach for it in attributing their conduct to their lives of faith, their regular worship and praise of God, their belonging to the Church and participation in its practices. If we retell their story in consequentialist terms we might make it sound more appealing to those secular hearers who want to see what tangible contribution churchgoers make to the communities in which they live, and who assess such contributions by reference to results and outputs rather than by reference to their intrinsic quality. But, in doing so, we fail to do justice to the lives of obedience lived by the Margarets of this world, and, perhaps more fundamentally, we risk losing our faith in the power of rural theology to make a distinctive contribution to our thinking about life in the countryside.

Social capital and the kingdom

Even stronger than the temptation to express the worth of the contribution made by churchgoers to rural communities in consequentialist terms is the temptation to use the language of 'social capital'. The research that informed *Faith in Rural Communities* was intended to reveal the substantial contribution made by rural churchgoers to the social capital of their communities. The report succeeded in doing this, and has been very useful in stimulating public debate about the Church's role in rural affairs. But the report is in danger of attempting to express the Church's role in rural life by reference to secular discourses – in this case, the discourse of social capital. I will argue that, while this might enable the Church to use language that secular hearers more readily understand than, say, the theological story I am telling about community, it represents a failure to do justice to the deep narrative of community that undergirds the life of Christian discipleship. It dilutes the distinctiveness of the contribution churchgoers make to life in the countryside. It tells, in other words, an incomplete story about what it means to be a Christian who is formed through participation in the Eucharist to love and serve his or her neighbours.

Social capital is a concept with origins in the social contractarianism of John Rawls's theory of justice, with which I engaged in Chapter 1. I stated there that Rawls's approach is unsatisfactory because, although it leads to a society of which fairness and equality are features, the means by which such features are arrived at rests upon a faulty anthropology. (By anthropology I mean the assumptions we make about human nature.) Rawls assumes that humans are self-interested individualists, whose primary concern is to look after self. Their motivation for participating in society, and ensuring its fairness and equality, resides in what Rawls assumes to be their self-interested response to the experience of going behind the 'veil of ignorance'. Participation in society is therefore only worthwhile because of what it can achieve for the individual, or, to put it differently, co-operation with fellow creatures is an instrumental good: we do it for what we can get out of it.

I have already rehearsed the basis of my belief that co-operation with one's fellow creatures has intrinsic worth, because it is the means by which we image the trinitarian God. It is our imaging of God that explains the fundamental difference between the Christian view of personhood and the one evidenced in Rawls's theory of justice. As Christians, we believe we are reconciled to God in a new creation, in which we recognize the importance of having a right relationship with the rest of creation and with one another. We are trained out of self-interest by our participation in the Eucharist, through which we learn our place in the drama of salvation history. We are shown the value of friendship through our breaking of bread and our sharing of wine, and we recognize that it is a struggle to live in wait for redemption, but that meanwhile we are welcome at Christ's table in all our frailty.

When social capital is used as an explanatory account of the motivation for participating in community, it allows no room for such a theological anthropology. Social capital is individualist in its assumptions. It assumes, like Rawls, that human beings co-operate only on the basis of the benefits that accrue to them as individuals as a result of so doing. Social capital offers a further step on from the Rawlsian theory of justice, in so far as it encourages far more than the minimal level of co-operation required to form the basis of the social contract. Proponents of social capital suggest that human beings should participate as fully as possible in the lives of their local communities and networks, because this is a means by which they can derive profound benefits for themselves. Social capital is the measure of these benefits – a community rich in social capital will be one where people co-operate to a high degree, while a community wanting for social capital will be one where co-operation between people is rare.

Robert Putnam wrote the seminal book about social capital, entitled *Bowling Alone*. The book was a bestseller in Putnam's native USA and in the UK, which perhaps reflects the hankering after community that I identified in the preceding chapter as a feature of modern life: a hankering that I have argued is pronounced among rural and would-be rural dwellers. Putnam's thesis is simple: he avers that American society has witnessed a breakdown in the bonds between people, evidenced by declining membership of sports clubs, associations and other networks. Putnam claims that the disintegration of social bonds has damaged American society, because co-operation between people yields benefits for all concerned, and the absence of such co-operation brings disadvantage. So, for example, he states that 'civic connections help make us healthy, wealthy, and wise'.[9] Putnam presents evidence to suggest that people whose lives are rich in social capital are better able to cope with traumatic experiences and illness.[10] He states that social capital increases people's employment prospects, enhances their safety and makes them better able to function in a just society.[11] Putnam suggests a link between social capital and the quality of children's education,[12] and he urges his readers therefore to 'reweave the fabric of [their] communities'.[13]

Putnam's findings have been amplified, proved and developed by subsequent authors with an interest in the concept of social capital.[14] This has inevitably led to disagreement about the precise definition of the term,[15] but most agree with Putnam that, if the accrual of social capital is to be encouraged, it is for the following reason: 'Networks of community engagement foster sturdy norms of reciprocity: I'll do this for you now, in the expectation that you (or perhaps someone else) will return the favour.'[16] Whether the expected comeback from community

---

9 Putnam, Robert, 2000, *Bowling Alone*, New York: Simon and Schuster, p. 287.

10 Putnam, *Bowling Alone*, p. 289.

11 Putnam, *Bowling Alone*, p. 290.

12 Putnam, *Bowling Alone*, p. 297.

13 Putnam, *Bowling Alone*, p. 402.

14 Field, John, 2003, *Social Capital*, London: Routledge.

15 Farrell *et al.*, *Faith in Rural Communities*, p. 14.

16 Putnam, *Bowling Alone*, p. 20.

engagement is specific (for example, mowing a neighbour's lawn on the basis that he will wash my car next Thursday), or more general (for example, fundraising for the local hospice, because I might need its care one day), the reason for engaging in community life is basically reducible to self-interest. Contributing to the life of one's local community, when expressed by reference to the concept of social capital, is ultimately self-serving, even when the associated benefits do not accrue directly to oneself in the short term.

Social capital is nowadays divided into three categories:

- bonding social capital, which functions by strengthening the bonds between members of small community groups, such as churches or football clubs;
- bridging social capital, which functions by improving bonds between different networks within a wider community, such as when a football club helps with the penalty shoot-out at the church fete; and
- linking social capital, which functions by connecting communities to one another, such as when the football teams of neighbouring villages play one another, or their church choirs join together for a concert.

The three categories relate to the distinctions made between the activities of churchgoers identified by *Faith in Rural Communities*, which I outlined near the start of this chapter. To recall, the report found that churchgoers contribute to their local communities by strengthening the bonds between community members (bonding capital, such as when a congregation member visits the elderly in their village), by joining a number of networks in addition to their involvement in the church (bridging capital, such as when a member of the church volunteers to help with the local reading club), and by networking with other organizations in the wider area (linking capital, such as when a church member joins the league of friends of the local cottage hospital).

Now I do not wish to deny that, when expressed in these terms, the Church's members make a profound contribution to the social capital of their communities. I agree with Michael Langrish's assertion that the Church plays a significant role in sustaining and developing the three types of social capital.[17] I applaud the *Faith in Rural Communities* project for unearthing so much information to support the idea that the Church and its members are contributing to their rural communities in manifold ways. But I urge that we resist the temptation to move from viewing social capital as a tool to describe what happens when churchgoers contribute to their local communities, to using it as a tool to explain why they are motivated to make such contributions. When social capital is used in the latter way, as Putnam and others assume it can be, then we end up telling a very different story about community from the theological one I have been exploring so far in this book. Rather than seeing community as a sign of the new creation, in which we have a right relationship with the non-human and human world around us, social capital accounts would have us believe that communities exist only because self-interested agents recognize that co-operation with others is the best way to get on in life. There may be many benefits that flow from contributing to the social capital of one's community, and the Church may well make a significant contribution to the accrual of bonding, bridging and linking capital. But such benefits are subsidiary, since, for Christian disciples, community is an end of itself: participation in the eucharistic life of the Church, from which we are sent to love and serve the Lord, is our motivation for contributing to

---

17 Langrish, Michael, 2004, 'Dynamics of Community', in Jeremy Martineau, Leslie Francis and Peter Francis (eds), *Changing Rural Life*, Norwich: Canterbury Press, pp. 33–6.

community life. The theological story of community is its own explanation, and it is a story that we live primarily for the good of the world.

A primer in rural theology

The remainder of this book represents my attempt to tell the story of contemporary rural life by reference to the narrative of Christian salvation history, by which the Church is constituted and in which it is sustained by the Holy Spirit, through its practice of the Eucharist. I hope to resist the temptation to dilute that story in order that it may sound more acceptable to secular ears. I cannot claim my telling of it to be complete, however: there are issues which do not receive sufficient treatment in subsequent chapters, and there are parts of rural life, such as pressure on rural housing, which do not receive any discussion whatever. But it is my hope that the attempt to offer a primer in rural theology, which has been the central activity of these opening chapters, will equip congregation members and their leaders to think seriously about what it means to play their part in the drama of Christ's saving work and to live in the new creation. I hope that the main thrust of my argument is plain: that if the Church gets its worshipping and liturgical life right, its ethical life will follow; that if church members are formed through participation in the Eucharist to share Christ's love and justice with the world, then they are uniquely placed to contribute to the lives of their rural communities in profound ways. And, fundamentally, that we come into God's presence at the Eucharist in all our frailty, as those who make mistakes and know we are forgiven, as Peter was forgiven by the Lord beside that charcoal fire at the Sea of Tiberias.

This way, we remind ourselves of the need to tread lightly in our engagement with the affairs of our wider communities, to take our shoes off before walking on the holy ground of our neighbours' lives. Our contribution to rural life might be distinctive, and we might believe ours to be the best story ever told about what it means to live in community with our fellow creatures. But our theological story also tells us that our judgements can be flawed, that God loves us for what we are, and that all are welcome at his table. We go to the world in peace, to love and serve the Lord.

4

Food and Farming

This chapter represents a shift in my focus. Having offered a primer to rural theology in the first three chapters, my attention now turns to particular issues affecting those who live in the countryside. I begin in this chapter by focusing on agriculture and, more fundamentally, on the relation of farming to life in rural communities. In the first section, before I look more closely at this topic, I briefly reflect on the proper role of rural theology when it comes to engaging with practical issues in rural life. Rural theology is an activity requiring of its participants that we be disciplined in what we say, and that we remain humbly aware of the limits of our knowledge and expertise. I am reminding myself that, in so far as the story I am telling in this book is theological, my engagement with key issues in rural life will be a theological engagement. I have no expertise in economics or politics, in agriculture or environmental science. What I say, therefore, is what I believe to be within my capabilities of saying, as one who is formed by a life of Christian worship, and who sees that such formation might make a difference to the ways in which those who have been similarly formed might interact with rural life.

When it comes to sharing Christ's love and justice with the rural communities of which we are a part, I make three points about what we might do in relation to farming and our consumption of food. These are made in the second and third sections of this chapter. First, I suggest that our primary responsibility is to extend the friendship that we are taught through our participation in the Eucharist to all of those who belong to the farming community. Too often, farmers can be isolated from the communities of which they are a part: those of us who seek to image the trinitarian God have a particular call to draw such people into our fellowship and friendship. Second and third, I address two particular issues relating to our consumption of the fruits of agriculture. I argue that a rural theology such as I am outlining is compatible with the decision by humans to eat meat, provided proper attention is paid to the manner in which live-stock is reared and slaughtered. Related to this, I suggest that the choices we make in terms of our purchase of farm produce are central to our imaging of God. In other words, if wherever possible we buy locally sourced produce from small-scale mixed farms, we can better engender a right relationship with both our human and our non-human neighbours.

On humility

Let me be clear: when I say, as I have done in the previous chapter, that the theological story I am telling about community 'out-narrates' secular discourses, I mean that assertion to have a spe-cific meaning. When it comes to thinking about community as a concept, the theological story in which we see ourselves as images of the trinitarian God, called to be Christlike through our partici-pation in the Eucharist and to share God's gifts with the world, is by far the best one going. Through the Eucharist, we are shown how to be friends, we are trained out of self-interest and we are reminded of our frailty as those who come before Christ's table and are ready to be forgiven. There can, it seems to me, be no bet-ter account of what it is to be human, to live as community with our brothers and sisters and to participate in the new creation.

Now it is clear that, as Christian disciples, we come to take certain things for granted. In the previous chapter I showed that churchgoing makes a difference to the way we behave in relation to our fellow creatures. And since Christ's life, death, resurrection and ascension are for the whole creation, as Paul reminds us in Romans 8, we clearly have something to say about all of God's economy. Theology is not an activity undertaken in a religious enclave; it intersects with every aspect of existence because it is fundamentally concerned with what it means to be a creature who is reconciled to God through Christ, sustained by the spirit, and longing for redemption.

As Tim Gorringe reminds us, the Eucharist intersects with every aspect of life, by bathing our 'daily reality in the light of the Triune God, teaching us that our lives and our world are gifts'.[1] In the Eucharist, mundane, worldly things – bread from the baker's, fermented grape juice – are brought before God and transformed, as we are, and as our world is. But simply imbibing that bread and wine does not give Christian disciples expertise in every aspect of human life. It does not equip us, say, with superior knowledge when it comes to matters of economics or politics. Quite the reverse, in fact; it reminds us of the fragility of our judgements, by showing us that God accepts us at his table in spite of them. The Eucharist teaches us humility in our interactions with the world we are called to serve. It reminds us that service requires that we listen and learn from our brothers and sisters who might be better placed than we are to make decisions about, for example, how they should conduct their businesses, which houses they should buy, or where they should send their children to school. Our role as Christ's disciples is to bring these worldly concerns to God's altar in the hope that they may be made sacred through our worship and praise of him.

To put it another way, the response of Christian disciples to worldly matters cannot be anything other than a theological

---

1 Gorringe, Timothy, 1997, *The Sign of Love: Reflections on the Eucharist*, London: SPCK, p. 4.

response. We cannot claim expertise in the social sciences or in agro-economics or local government – unless, by some chance, we happen to have a professional interest in such areas. So our contribution to rural life is a contribution born out of our participation in the life of the Church, through which we are formed to image the trinitarian God. Rural theology is the activity of Christians responding to the issues facing people who live in the countryside in ways that are Christlike, and therefore are primarily oriented to the good of the world around them. In other words, the proper questions for rural theology to ask relate to the ways in which Christ's love and justice can be made known far and wide among rural dwellers. Rural theology will not try to tell a farmer how to manage his land, therefore, or a headteacher how to lead her school. Rather, it will ask how Christian disciples can interact with the farmer and the headteacher in ways that image God who is Trinity, in whose new creation we are called to have a right relationship with our fellow creatures.

A recent history of British agriculture

Only 0.3 per cent of the UK's population works directly in agriculture, and yet those people care for 70 per cent of our land-mass.[2] That is a big responsibility being shared by a tiny number of people, who work long and unsocial hours and are extremely vulnerable to economic hardship. The past decade has seen farming begin to emerge from a sustained period of crisis, in which revenues plummeted, confidence in British food faltered and many farmers simply went out of business. The acrid smoke of the foot-and-mouth funeral pyres that were scattered across

---

2 For a more detailed account of British agriculture than the one offered here, see Anthony J. Russell, 'Farming in a Time of Transition', in Jeremy Martineau, Leslie Francis and Peter Francis (eds), *Changing Rural Life*, Norwich: Canterbury Press, 2004, pp. 156–75.

our countryside in 2001 continues to cast a pall over many rural areas, long after the television cameras and newspaper reports have disappeared. And while many farmers have actually benefited from generous compensation as a result of the crisis, with some receiving millions of pounds to replace dead stock,[3] the emotional turmoil of the episode has left deep scars. The foot-and-mouth outbreak was one of three significant crises to affect farming over a period from the late 1980s to the early 2000s in which the whole industry struggled for survival. The economic damage sustained over this time is only part of the story: another considerable cost is the impact on farmers' morale.

Foot-and-mouth tended to bring the general public out in support of farmers, with many expressing sympathy for those whose livelihoods could be seen, quite literally, going up in smoke on television screens across the country. The same cannot be said of the two other major crises, salmonella and BSE. In 1988, Edwina Currie infamously commented on national television that most eggs laid on British farms were infected with salmonella. Currie's remarks were ill-informed, since of the 30 million eggs consumed per year at the time, only 26 cases of salmonella had been reported. To counter the Junior Health Secretary's statement, the British Egg Industry Council observed that the chance of eating an egg infected with salmonella was around 200 million to 1. As outbreaks go, this one was kept fairly well in check. But the damage was done, and UK consumers steered clear of eggs, sending producers into chaos, and leaving them feeling abandoned by their customers.

A similar story can be told about the BSE crisis, which started in 1996. A suggestion of a link between the degenerative Creutzfeldt–Jakob Disease (CJD) in humans and the cattle disease BSE was publicized, and the market for British beef dropped like a stone.

---

3 'Foot and Mouth payouts are too high, says former NFU economist', *Guardian*, 7 August 2001.

Leading supermarket chains took British beef off their shelves, a European export ban was imposed on beef from British farms, and consumers once again voted with their wallets, avoiding domestic meat in favour of products from Europe, South America and the USA. The EU ban on British beef was only lifted in 2006, bringing to an end ten of the hardest years that cattle farmers have ever endured.

The years of the late twentieth and early twenty-first centuries were by no means easy for any sector of British agriculture. World commodity prices slumped by almost 50 per cent, meaning that farmers' profit margins were squeezed until they became non-existent. In 2002, pig farmers were losing about £3 per pig sold at market. Sheep farmers fared even worse, with their costs of production far outstripping the prices of their beasts at auction. The average farm-gate price of milk dropped to historically low levels, dipping well below 16 pence per litre from highs of over 25 pence per litre in the early 1990s. Ironically, given the nation's aversion to all things chicken-related after the salmonella controversy, the poultry industry was one of the few farming sectors that flourished in the 1990s. Even here, though, the drive for cheap supermarket chickens was already putting downward pressure on prices, and setting the foundations of an animal welfare time-bomb that has only just exploded in the minds of many consumers.

If livestock farmers were beleaguered, things were no better for their counterparts in arable farming. In profitability terms, this sector was worse off than the livestock industry: by 2002, the Department for the Environment, Food and Rural Affairs – Defra – estimated that arable farms were making just 10 per cent of the profit they enjoyed in the early 1990s, compared to 30 per cent for livestock farmers. Overall, farmers earned 40 per cent less in 1999 than they did in 1990, despite the economy having gone through a period of high inflation and the strong pound having weakened the export market. The relative value of subsidies, on which so many farming businesses depend for their continued survival, had also been considerably reduced.

It is little wonder, therefore, that in 2002, an estimated 1,000 people a week were leaving the agricultural sector in search of other work. This exodus was driven partly by economic necessity, and partly by the disaffection of farmers and farm workers with the industry in which they were struggling to make a living. In consequence, farming became an increasingly solitary activity. Those who remained on the land found themselves working in isolation, just at a time when companionship and reassurance from colleagues were most needed. Set against this background, the fact that farmers have one of the highest suicide rates in the country is hardly surprising. At its worst, in 1999, farmers were two-and-a-half times more likely to take their own lives than an average worker in the UK. The current figure is not much lower.

The nub of the problem facing farmers at the turn of the century was identified in a report produced for the government by a commission led by Sir Don Curry, entitled *Farming and Food: A Sustainable Future*. In the course of his survey of the industry, Curry noted that hardly anyone to whom his commission spoke had a good word to say about the state of British agriculture.[4] Curry sensed that farmers felt 'disconnected' and 'detached' from the rest of the economy and environment, and from the communities in which they lived.[5] The detachment of farmers from their communities is a two-way problem, since it also leads to ignorance and impatience of the industry among people whose lives are not intimately bound up with it. It is disconcerting, for example, to discover that one child in every twenty thinks that chips and chicken kievs come ready-made from the fields, or that one in three thinks that if cows eat grass it will turn their milk

---

4 Curry, Sir Don, 2002, *Farming and Food: A Sustainable Future*, London: HMSO, p. 13.

5 Curry, *Farming and Food*, p. 6.

green. But at least these children know where milk comes from – 6 per cent of those questioned could not even tell researchers that much.[6] More worrying is the finding of the Archbishops' Commission, when researching *Faith in the Countryside*, that rural dwellers might subject local farmers to abuse because they do not understand the rhythms and patterns of agricultural life.[7]

Bearing in mind what I have said about the role of rural theology as being principally concerned with the places where our eucharistic life intersects with the daily concerns of the community around us, the isolation of farmers seems to be a serious consideration. If farmers are disconnected from those around them, and feel that disconnection keenly, then it is surely incumbent upon those who participate in the worshipping life of the Church, more than anyone else, to extend bonds of friendship and fellowship to the farmers in our midst. It is part of our imaging of the trinitarian God to think creatively about ways in which we can make Christ's love and justice known among these people.

Beyond the farm gate

Behind the farm gate there is human drama. Farmers are wives and husbands, mothers and fathers, sons and daughters, just as they are those whom we entrust to care for our natural environment and put food on our plates. They suffer from illness and depression, from short tempers and frayed nerves. They have anxieties and hopes, fears and aspirations. They share laughter and joy, and welcome the warmth of fellowship. When we

---

6 This research was carried out in April 2007 by TNS Online Kids Omnibus, as part of a publicity campaign by the dairy co-operative Dairy Farmers of Britain.

7 ACORA, 1990, *Faith in the Countryside*, Worthing: Churchman Publishing, p. 63; see also Sally Gaze, 2006, *Mission-Shaped and Rural*, London: Church House Publishing, p. 21.

trace the hard times of farming, we are talking not only of the economic hardships that come from trying to make a living in a struggling industry, but about the hardships that come from a sense of isolation, from a loss of faith in our ability to fulfil our vocation. For, as evidenced by the number of elderly farmers who ploughed their foot-and-mouth compensation straight back into their herds, rather than shutting up shop and settling down to retirement,[8] farming is nothing if not a vocation. When our lives become disconnected from those of the people around us, we can struggle to feel God's love; his image in us can be hard to discern.

So, if rural theology has something to say about farming, then its focus lies first where the Eucharist intersects with the lives of the men and women whose hands toil in the ground so that we might have food to eat. Economically, things have begun to look more positive for British agriculture in recent years. The weaker pound of the financial crisis in 2009 has inflated the relative value of subsidies. Renewed interest among consumers in food provenance has improved profitability among some suppliers. Arable prices have increased gradually, aided by demand for crops that can be turned into biofuels. But to assume that better business prospects tell the whole story is to ignore the human cost of those years of crisis. The new creation is one in which our principal concern is on the nature of the relationships shared between humans, and between humans and the rest of the created order. Reconnecting farmers to their communities is about enabling them to participate in such relationships; it is about reaching out in friendship as those who have been formed by the Eucharist.

That is not to assume that many farmers are not already intimately involved in the lives of their local churches, or that they

---

8 Southgate, Christopher, 2008, *The Groaning of Creation*, Louisville: Westminster John Knox Press, p. 119.

do not participate in its Eucharist and become transformed in the sharing of bread and wine. It is certainly true, anyway, that many farmers have a notional commitment to the local church, and are happy to help in ways such as maintaining the upkeep of church buildings, or by offering tractor rides at the parish fete. In this regard, farmers are no different from many other rural dwellers.[9] But we can, and must, do more to make Christ's love and justice known to these people who, by their own admission, feel separated from their local communities.

One very practical way in which to share friendship with farmers and farm workers is to ensure that they are included in the visiting rotas of our churches, so that they might be included in the wider community of fellowship that the Eucharist engenders. Farmers are busy people, but they are often to be found close to their homes, and even the briefest of conversations with a member of the church will help to make them feel connected to the community beyond the farm gate. It can be surprising what arises from such encounters. For example, the farmer or farm worker might find that there is a project being undertaken by the church with which they can lend a hand, or the visitor might discover that the farmer could do with some help on his or her land for an hour or so, and find volunteers from the church or wider community to assist. Farming is a way of life that many people find fascinating, and becoming involved in the manual work of agriculture can be theologically revealing. It can remind us of our God-given role in creation as tillers and keepers of the land (Gen. 2.15). To work the land can be a profoundly religious experience, reminding us of our intimacy with the created world and of our need to nurture a right relationship with it. The opportunity for the Church's worshipping community to become involved in the

---

9 Savigear, Elfrida, 1999, 'The Local Community', in Jeremy Martineau (ed.), *Bridging the Gap: The Church in the Local Community*, Stoneleigh: ACORA Publishing, pp. 12–13.

activities of local farmers is one that ought to be grasped, for such work will certainly connect us to the drama of salvation history.

Even better, churches might choose to gather for worship on local farms from time to time, praising God and giving thanks for his gifts in a context where many of those gifts are plainly seen. This would show farmers that they belong to the community, that they have their own place in the drama of salvation history and that the worshipping Church is with them, alongside them, and encouraging them in their work. Farmers find it notoriously difficult to attend church services, because the rhythms of their working day are often out of kilter with the church's timetable. It would make a marvellous statement to farmers if that timetable could occasionally be adjusted, even if the implied invitation to attend church is not accepted. Simply knowing that the church prizes their contribution to the community sufficiently to make this step would be a fine way of showing Christlike love and friendship to them. And, perhaps, when a farm is visited or a farmer seen round about, he or she can be reminded that the Church prays with them and for them: when we are lonely, it is a comfort to know that others hold us in their prayers.

I am suggesting that rural theology requires us to remind farmers of their connection to local communities, and that doing so flows from the Church's eucharistic practice. My suggestion might seem to be romantic, perhaps even quaint. But friendship is at the core of our existence, as those who are called to a right relationship with one another and with the rest of creation. The Eucharist shows us how to be friends. If the Church cannot tell farmers how to sow their crops or breed their cattle, it can at least show them what it means to live in community. For that is where the Church's story is more persuasive than the secular alternatives; that is where the resources of theology can out-narrate the resources of the secular world. So if we cannot extend friendship to the farming community in this time of fragility and recovery from crisis, and always, then we cannot have faith in rural theology.

Some might respond to these suggestions by saying that they promulgate an unrealistic view of agriculture. After all, much of the agricultural industry in the UK is nowadays made up of large-scale intensive farms, where workers – often migrants – are employed on a piecemeal basis and the operation is slick, impersonal and geared towards the maximizing of profits. I shall say more about our ethical response to such practices in what follows below, but it is enough, I think, to remind ourselves that on these farms, as on smaller operations, people live and work, and will need friendship. We would not expect an industrial chaplain to avoid visiting a large factory simply because of the scale of its operation, or to assume that the managing director of a large corporation might not be as much in need of the love and justice of Christ as the lone shopkeeper. Nor should we expect, therefore, that those who farm on a large scale need our friendship any less than those who operate smaller holdings. The detail of our pastoral care of such people might adjust, our strategies might be different in response to their different ways of life. But our call to be Christlike and extend friendship to them obtains whatever the scale of their operations. That is what I mean when I say that the Eucharist shows us how to be friends. It reminds us that at the heart of our communities are people, whose human dramas can find a place within the larger drama of God's redemptive work.

We are what we eat

When we think about farming, we are invited to think more deeply about the origins of our food. The Eucharist shows us that what we put in our mouths matters: when we think about the intersection of the Eucharist with food and farming, we might well address the question of what we should and should not eat. Since rural theology requires us to have a right relationship with the rest of creation as well as with one another, the question of the moral status of meat consumption seems to be at the heart of our considerations. I suggest that eating meat, when it is enabled by the careful rearing and slaughter of livestock, can be truly eucharistic, in so far as it is an extension of the possibility of relationship between the species.

On this subject, I tend to agree with the position elucidated by Chris Southgate in *The Groaning of Creation*. Southgate argues:

> [T]he breeding, rearing and management of animals in the context of healthy methods of farming (including genuinely humane killing) can be considered a form of care and friendship between species that is an authentic part of the human vocation, part indeed that extends the possibilities of relationship between species, and is therefore not to be abandoned as part of the pursuit of an eschatological ethic.[10]

The arguments against such a position rest in a belief, expressed by Andrew Linzey, that the new creation is one in which non-human creatures are released from futility, pain and worthlessness (a view he derives from Romans 8.19–21).[11] Linzey would assert that the belief that humans can rear, and subsequently kill, other creatures is inherently anthropocentric – that is, it assumes that human interests are at the heart of God's redemptive project, rather than redemption being concerned with creation as a whole, as I argued in Chapter 1. The rejection of anthropocentrism has been important in the approach I have been arguing for, which sees right relationship between the human and non-human world as central to the drama of salvation history.

The question, then, is about what it means for humans to have a right relationship with the rest of creation – in particular, those

10 Southgate, *Groaning of Creation*, p. 121.
11 Linzey, Andrew, 1994, *Animal Theology*, London: SCM Press.

creatures that we have tended to breed, rear and slaughter to eat. Following Southgate, I suggest that the meaning of the prohibitions in Acts 15.29, which require abstinence from 'food sacrificed to idols, strangled animals and blood', can be interpreted as an injunction to eat only animals that have been appropriately cared for and killed in a humane fashion. I am persuaded by Southgate's assertion that

> all animals killed within a process which has no care for their wellbeing, but regards them only as commodities to be 'manufactured' as cheaply as possible, transported wherever necessary, and killed only with concern for efficiency and not the relief of distress, have been sacrificed to the idol of human economic efficiency.

What is more, I agree with his view that the constraint on strangling and blood is a 'requirement for humane killing and careful butchery'.[12] If Acts 15.29, so interpreted, is our guide, then right relationship between creatures is constituted by an appropriate attitude of care and respect in our handling of animals bred for human consumption. Indeed, the advice given to Christians at the Council of Jerusalem might well offer a helpful basis for something like a Christian ethical code of animal husbandry, by which Christian farmers and butchers could be encouraged to conduct their businesses. What it certainly means is that a prohibition on meat-eating, on grounds that it involves inappropriate human dominance over the non-human world, and therefore damages the relation between humans and the rest of creation, can be easily rebuffed.

Perhaps harder to dismiss is the argument that eating meat, and red meat in particular, is damaging our environment and

---

12 Southgate, *Groaning of Creation*, p. 121.

exacerbating climate change. It is easily said that one can drive a 4×4 many times around the planet before equalling the annual greenhouse emissions of a 200-acre beef farm. Less glib, but more insightful, are calculations that raise serious concerns about the carbon footprint of methane-producing animals like sheep and cattle, since methane is a potent gas, causing more damage gram for gram than equivalent carbon dioxide emissions.[13] A food chain predicated upon the intensive breeding, rearing and slaughtering of methane-producing beasts for human consumption might therefore seem to be ill-advised; vegetarianism might be less a spiritual choice and more a practical means of preserving the planet.

First, it is worth reminding ourselves of the need to resist anthropocentrism, lest the argument just propounded in favour of meat-avoidance is read as a concern principally for human well-being. Second, it should be noted that crop growth relies upon nutrients that are found either in manure or in environmentally damaging chemical fertilizers. Third, we might note that all but the most locally grown and seasonal vegetables and cereals involve significant production of greenhouse gases in their planting, growth, harvesting and transportation. Fourth, we do well to observe that many parts of the UK in particular are unsuitable for arable use, and would therefore be incapable of providing food for local markets if they were not used as pasture. Fifth, it hardly needs saying that many rare species are protected by virtue of their place in the food chain, and would become extinct if agricultural practices did not preserve them. And sixth, it is worth reminding ourselves of the environmental desecration caused by the fighting of wars, the practices of global business, and the production of consumer goods like mobile telephones, computers and motor vehicles. In other words, while the argument that

13 Morrison, Reg, 1999, *The Spirit in the Gene*, Ithaca, NY: Cornell University Press, p. 23, quoted in Southgate, *Groaning of Creation*, p. 181.

vegetarianism is a means of arresting climate change might seem compelling, it is also rather naive.

Small is beautiful

Meat production can be a part of the maintenance of a right relationship between humans and the non-human world. Good husbandry, a genuine concern for animal welfare, and humane slaughter can be a means of extending the relationship between species. Such a process might even be described as 'sacramental'.[14] But herein lies the rub, for the argument I am outlining rests upon an assumption concerning the type of farming that produces meat for human consumption. And my rebuttal of the argument that vegetarianism is a means of reducing our contribution to climate change rests upon a similar assumption. This is namely that meat is produced on small-scale farms, preferably with mixed stock and a balance between arable and livestock. Timothy Gorringe offers a powerful argument for such an approach in his book about food and farming, and he identifies several benefits that accrue from small-scale mixed farming in comparison to large-scale intensive methods. These include:

- limiting the spread of disease;
- greater recycling of waste because, for example, manure can be used to fertilize crops grown on the same farm;
- the generation of benefits for the wider natural environment, because mixed farms are more likely to utilize labour-intensive practices such as hedge-laying, which help maintain biodiversity;

---

14 Berry, Wendell, 1981, *The Gift of the Good Land: Further Essays Cultural and Agricultural*, San Francisco: North Point Press, p. 281.

- an enhancement to the lives of rural communities, because mixed farms tend to employ more people; and
- a more efficient use of energy sources, because of a reduced reliance on mechanization in comparison to intensive farming methods.[15]

James Jones echoes many of Gorringe's sentiments in his essay about the origins of food in *Changing Rural Lives*.[16]

There is a precedent, therefore, among theologians for favouring small-scale mixed farms over large-scale intensive set-ups. Such an approach is in keeping with my rebuttal of the two arguments used to suggest that vegetarianism is a requirement of the life of discipleship. On small farms, the relationship between farmer and livestock can be more intimate, more sacramental, than on a large-scale farm in which the rearing of beasts is akin to a food production line. What is more, small farms will keep fewer livestock, bringing an automatic reduction in methane production per farm. And, because of the cyclical approach to farming that is facilitated by a mixed holding, manure can be used in place of chemical fertilizers that harm the environment in other ways. Mixed farms might also enable a more complete embodying of community, and are therefore to be commended in the new creation.

What does this mean for the rural church member who is concerned to share Christ's love and justice with their local community, and be in right relationship with one another and with the rest of creation? I have already said that it is not the place of theologians to tell other specialists about their work. I do not think it would be a Christlike act to castigate those farmers who run large-scale intensive operations, for reasons I have

---

15 Gorringe, Timothy, 2006, *Harvest: Food, Farming and the Churches*, London: SPCK, pp. 101–5.

16 Jones, James, 2004, 'Eating Well', in Martineau, Francis and Francis (eds), *Changing Rural Life*, p. 159.

already outlined concerning what the Eucharist shows us about the importance of friendship. But rural churchgoers who wish to take their place in the drama of salvation history can embody a commitment to small-scale mixed agriculture in a simple way: by changing our habits when it comes to what we eat. I believe that the Eucharist trains us into new habits, which enable us to better image the trinitarian God. Practically speaking, one aspect of such imaging might be that we consciously support those farmers who sell their produce in the local market, rather than buy globally sourced food from supermarket chains. Nowadays there are many opportunities to buy locally and to eat seasonally, and they should be taken with relish by those of us who have a concern for the nature of our relationship with our fellow creatures. Such food is most likely to have been produced in a fashion that honours and advances the relationship between different species, and it will also most likely have come from a mixed farm.

Additionally, shopping locally brings us into direct contact with the people who toil to produce the food we eat. It is a further means by which we can extend friendship to the members of the farming community in our midst, as well as providing tangible evidence of our belief in the virtue of what they do. I believe that rural churches should think seriously about providing space for farmers to sell their produce on a regular basis – in the church hall, for example, or even in the church itself. Another helpful practical suggestion might be that churches publish details of local farmers' markets and farm shops to be distributed with the parish magazine. And, of course, on an individual basis, churchgoers can choose to shop locally wherever possible, thereby training themselves into a Christlike habit.

When Christian disciples find their place in the drama of salvation history through participation in the Eucharist, they are called to share Christ's love and justice with the world. In thinking about the origins of our food, and remembering that what we put in our mouths matters in a profound way to our life in the new creation, we are able to find exciting opportunities to connect with the farmers in our local communities. Rural theology offers an encouragement to churchgoers to extend friendship to local farmers who, by their own admission, feel isolated from their wider communities. Rural theology also indicates ways in which we might be trained, through participation in the Eucharist, to think more carefully about what we eat. Good husbandry, and responsible farming practices in general, are central in the right relation of the human to the non-human world. In training its members to make Christlike choices about how we eat, and how we source what we eat, the rural church can be a Eucharist for the world it is called to serve.

5

The Church and Rural Services

In this chapter, I argue that a primary practical concern of rural theology, and therefore rural church members, is to build community. To this end, those of us who are formed by the Eucharist to take our place in the drama of salvation history are called to involvement in the wider communities of which we are a part. The lives of love and service to which we are sent after sharing Christ's body and blood involve participation in community life in our villages and hamlets, in ways that make Christ's love and justice known to them. One of the central ways in which this can be achieved is by church members taking an interest in rural services. As I shall argue, vibrant rural communities are centred on vibrant services like schools, pubs, village shops and post offices. Rural theology has a particular concern with these services because it has a concern with the idea of community as an intrinsic good, participation in which reflects our imaging of the trinitarian God. If the Church believes it has the best story to tell concerning community, and that story teaches us that life in community is God-given, then it is central to the Church's calling that it helps to facilitate flourishing communities wherever it is present.

One of the key ways in which the Church can facilitate vibrant community life is through involvement in rural schools. Support for rural schools provides a particular opportunity for the Church to live its story concerning community, and involvement in the life of rural schools should be taken seriously as a particular vocation for some church members. Healthy schools embody community, and they can contribute to community flourishing by providing places of learning and formation for young and old alike. Active participation in the life of local schools is central to the activity of rural theology. What is more, church schools, of which there are many in the countryside, provide a particular opportunity for the Church to help people take their place in the drama of salvation history.

At the end of this chapter, I discuss the importance of other rural services to life in the countryside, arguing that community flourishing is predicated upon the vibrancy of some of these services. I note the government's commitment to rural service provision, and offer an argument in which rural dwellers are encouraged by the Church to make use of the services in their midst that contribute to community life. I also suggest that rural churches might consider taking an active role in rural service provision as an aspect of a Eucharist-informed ministry of friendship in the community.

The importance of schools in rural communities

Faith in the Countryside recognizes that schools often lie at the heart of rural life, as institutions that embody the culture and values of a place and contribute to a strong feeling of community.[1] When rural inhabitants are asked about the services that matter most to them, schools feature high in the list along with pubs, village shops, churches and village halls.[2] Their importance in community life is signalled in the widespread anger in places

---

1 ACORA, 1990, *Faith in the Countryside*, Worthing: Churchman Publishing, p. 104.

2 Langrish, Michael, 2006, 'Seeds in Holy Ground – A Future for the Rural Church? A Background Briefing from the Mission and Public Affairs Council', Warwick: ARC, p. 8.

threatened with school closures, where residents feel as if they risk losing far more than a place in which to educate their children.[3] Schools are places for the whole community, which can provide a focus for a wide range of activities from sports clubs to craft classes and which serve a valuable role in building and sustaining community.

According to the Commission for Rural Communities, the number of school closures has fallen in recent years, from around 34 per year in the mid 1990s to more like 5 per year in the past decade. This reflects a policy by the Labour government elected to power in 1997 to protect rural schools from closure wherever possible. But even though they have official protection from closure, the diminutive size of most rural schools means that they have a hard job to remain vibrant and flourishing. Often, with relatively small staff teams carrying a disproportionate administrative load alongside full-time teaching responsibilities, rural schools can only succeed with help from volunteers in the local community.[4] Church members, who are formed through their participation in the Eucharist to image the trinitarian God, might feel a special vocation to serve their local schools, on grounds that by doing so they can help build community in the areas in which they live.

In 1996, the National Society published a booklet entitled *Churches Serving Schools*, which David Lankshear regards as a useful resource in helping the rural church to think about its contribution to the vibrancy of local schools. The booklet suggests five ways in which churches can serve the schools in their midst: prayer, befriending, positive support, welcome ministries, and freeing members for service. In each case, it seems to me,

---

3 ACORA, *Faith in the Countryside*, p. 109.

4 Lankshear, David, 1999, 'Church and School: Serving the Community', in Jeremy Martineau (ed.), *Bridging the Gap: The Church in the Local Community*, Stoneleigh: ACORA Publishing, p. 15.

rural churches could view adherence to the National Society's advice as properly eucharistic. Using Lankshear's discussion in *Bridging the Gap* as a primer, I offer five principles that might govern the rural church's involvement in local schools.

The rural church should pray for its local school

In the previous chapter, I suggested that church members might pray for local farmers as a sign of their friendship to them. Similarly, local schools should feature in the prayer cycles of rural churches, since as Christians we believe that praying makes a difference to the world around us. Our praying shows schools that they matter to us, because they are a part of the community we are called to serve. If representatives of the local school recognize that we hold them in our minds when we are engaged in the very activity that is most important to us, that they are at the heart of our worshipping life, then it shows them the degree of our commitment to their doings. Additionally – as I suggested in my brief discussion of the idea of liturgical reasoning in Chapter 2 – remembering the school in our prayers might crystallize our thinking about its life and activities. Church members might find that praying for the school brings practical wisdom in their thinking about the school's strategies, activities and overall governance.

One exciting opportunity for showing the school its importance in the church's prayer life is offered by Education Sunday. This ecumenical event has traditionally been held on the ninth Sunday before Easter, and it represents an opportunity for the Church to celebrate and pray for the work of everyone involved in education. A range of resources is available on the internet to support churches wishing to plan for the occasion,[5] and it might

---

5 http://www.cte.org.uk/Groups/64495/Churches_Together_in/Themes/ Social_Concern/Education/Churches_Schools/Education_Sunday.aspx (accessed March 2010).

provide an opportunity not only to pray *for* the local school, but to pray *with* it. Rather than viewing this as an activity which is principally geared towards church growth, it should be seen as an opportunity to show the school that church members give thanks for it, and recognize its importance to community life. Education Sunday might be conceived as a chance to hold a big 'thank you' party for the local school, which also provides an opportunity to celebrate its achievements, pray about its concerns, and offer worshipful support for it in God's presence. That such an event would almost certainly help to foster closer links between churches and their local schools is surely a good thing, because it has the potential to bring two groups, who in their own ways embody community for the good of the wider rural community, into closer co-operation with one another.

The rural church should extend friendship to its local school

The Eucharist shows us how to be friends. One of the central ways in which the lives of those who are formed through participation in the Eucharist intersect with the communities around them is in personal relationships. Church members are called to extend friendship to the people they meet, and with whom they share Christ's love and justice. Unlike members of the farming community, who, as I explored in the previous chapter, often feel isolated from their communities, rural schools have an integral place in the communities they are located in. But because friendship is part of Christian formation through worship, the interaction of church members with local schools is properly characterized by a reaching out in friendship to all those involved in the school's life – teachers, parents, pupils, governors and support staff. Lankshear talks about the need for clergy and others who work formally on behalf of the Church to develop friendly relationships with local schools,[6] but I would like to extend his suggestion to include all of those who are formed through involvement in the Church's worshipping life. This friendship is not directed to the aim of integrating the Church into the life of the school so much as to the aim of showing friendship to other members of our rural communities. Through such friendship, schools might be encouraged to work alongside the Church in sharing community more widely – but the hope is friendship first and foremost; any benefits that accrue from such relationships are secondary, and must not be allowed to drive our motivations. When such benefits become the motivating factor in closer working between churches and rural schools, Christians can easily end up reinforcing the consequentialist and social capital understandings of community that I rebutted in the third chapter, and which seems to me to be a poorer story about community than the one that we learn through participation in the Eucharist.

The rural church should offer positive support to its local school

Contemporary education is a challenging and complex arena: one that puts considerable pressure on people who work in it, and on pupils and students. Local schools are subject to routine inspections for quality assurance purposes, and are among many victims of a bureaucratic obsession with target-setting that has come to proliferate in the public sector. Such pressures can leave many school staff feeling vulnerable and highly sensitive to perceived criticism. When, as Lankshear warns, 'uninformed or unthinking' (but potentially well-meaning) people in the local community offer opinions about the school's life, this can be extremely damaging to the whole community.[7] Church members can seek to lessen this risk in two ways: first, by exercising

6 Lankshear, 'Church and School', p. 15.
7 Lankshear, 'Church and School', p. 16.

appropriate discipline in what they say about the school themselves, humbly recognizing that they might not have the right
expertise to fully understand the complexities of its life (a position I have seen as key to rural theology, as I explained at the
start of the preceding chapter); and second, by offering proactive
and positive support to the school wherever possible. This can
involve active participation in school events – sports days and
nativity plays, say, and fundraising activities – and it can also be
reflected in a general attitude of prayerful encouragement to the
school. Such positive support is Christlike, and should flow easily
enough from the two principles outlined above.

*The rural church should exercise a ministry of welcome to its
local school*

Churches are fascinating buildings, rich in history and often
holding great artistic and architectural treasures. They are places
where people can learn about the history of faith, about church
teaching and the Bible, about the seasons and patterns of the
liturgical year. They are places where people can come to learn
about praying and worshipping God, about music and hymnody,
about bell-ringing and tapestry-weaving. In short, churches are
among some of the most interesting buildings in the world, and
whether people are religious or not, they can gain a great deal
from visiting them. This point has been explored in some detail
by Sir Roy Strong in his *A Little History of the English Country
Church*.[8] Strong tells a powerful story about our fascination with
churches, and reminds his readers of their significance down the
centuries as places of education, formation and learning.

What this means is that most rural schools – primary and
secondary – have a treasure trove of learning available in their

---

8 Strong, Roy, 2008, *A Little History of the English Country Church*, London: Vintage Books.

immediate vicinity. A visit to the church, as Lankshear states, could be relevant to the study of art, RE, music, English literature or history.[9] And if the church, by flinging open its doors and welcoming the local school into its midst, can widen its ministry among local people, then that provides a further way in which its presence in the community can truly be said to be eucharistic. For the church's architecture, its stained-glass windows and rood screens tell the story of salvation history on which the lives of its people are centred. The church itself bears witness to Christ's love and justice, to God's promise to creation. Welcoming children and young people into these places is a sign that everyone is involved in the drama of salvation history, that the whole of creation is caught up in Christ's saving work.

So I advocate a ministry of welcome by church members to the local school. I hope the rural church sees that opening its doors for the purposes of furthering education among the young people in its community is one of the most significant acts of witness to Christ's love and justice available. No amount of outreach can speak as loudly as the message that this place, where we do the things that matter to us most, is open to all, and that we will do all we can to show hospitality and welcome to those who come here to learn about our stories. So far as the rural theology I am outlining in this book is concerned, the Church's openness to visitors reveals more about its eucharistic life than any other activity.

The rural church should free members to help its local school

In Chapter 3, I outlined the variety of ways in which church members make a profound contribution to the lives of their local communities, using the research published in *Faith in Rural Communities* as a guide. I argued that we should see the involvement

---

9 Lankshear, 'Church and School', p. 16.

of church members in community life as a feature of their imaging of the trinitarian God, rather than seeking to reduce such involvement to a weighing of its consequences, or to the idea of social capital. Christian disciples help build community because it is part of their place in the drama of salvation history, in which they are required to have a right relationship with the rest of creation and with one another. They do not contribute to community because they think it will lead to benefits, either for themselves or other people; community has intrinsic, rather than merely instrumental, value.

It is time-consuming to participate fully in the life of the Church, let alone in the life of the wider community. Voluntary work is just as demanding as paid employment, and it can lead to pressures on home and family life. Yet the theological story I am telling about community in this book encourages the Church's members to become as involved as possible in activities that build community in their local areas – that being the main argument of this chapter. In order to give members the space to participate in activities beyond the church, such as involvement in the life of the school, I echo Lankshear's advice that the Church should be willing to free its members from church-related responsibilities.[10] It might be that a member of the congregation has a far greater vocation to serve on the school's board of governors than on the PCC. Or it could be that a lay reader sees his or her call primarily in terms of volunteering to help the local school with its literacy schemes, rather than to preaching and teaching solely in the church context. The Church needs to see such work as part of its own mission and ministry. It is, after all, a primary means through which Christian disciples can image the God who is Trinity, by building community in ways that reflect the new creation. By freeing its members from church matters, in order that they may serve the local school more effectively, the

10 Lankshear, 'Church and School', p. 16.

Church embodies the other principles I have been outlining in this discussion concerning its relation to local schools. But, more fundamentally, it shows that being Christlike involves engagement in the wider community, that Christ's love and justice are for everyone.

Church schools

I have argued so far in this chapter that the rural church needs to become as involved as possible in the life of its local schools, showing prayerful friendship and support for its people, and helping it to build community in whatever ways are possible. Schools are a valuable resource for the whole community in the countryside, as Anthony Hodgson has remarked: 'A school is an institution concerned with education, formal and informal, of the whole community, developing lifelong learning opportunities for the personal and collective growth and development of the people it serves.'[11] Such an approach lies at the heart of the view of schools I have been advocating, and it obtains in particular in relation to church schools. There are approximately 4,700 Church of England schools in England, and many more schools supported by other Christian denominations, including 60 Methodist-maintained schools (of which half are run in partnership with the Church of England) and around 2,000 Roman Catholic schools. Like other denominations, the Church of England sees its schools as integral to the life and ministry of the parish church, rather than as mere 'add-ons'.[12] What is more, as Alan Smith notes, many of these schools are located in rural

---

11 Hodgson, Anthony, 1989, 'Work with Youth', in Rural Theology Association (RTA), *The Rural Church Towards 2000*, Northamptonshire: RTA, p. 102.

12 House of Bishops of the Church of England, 2001, *The Way Ahead: Church of England Schools in the New Millennium*, London: Church House Publishing, p. 53.

areas, where the Church of England has a historic role in the education of children and young people.[13] When we talk about rural schools, therefore, many such schools will be linked to the Church, and the type of involvement I have been describing so far in this chapter of church members in school life will be enshrined in their governance and staffing policies.

There is a distinction between church schools that are described as 'voluntary controlled' and those that are 'voluntary aided'. The former allow for less input by the Church in relation to religious education and governance, in exchange for reduced financial responsibility. The latter give the Church control over religious education as well as the right to appoint a majority of governors, with accompanying responsibility for the school's finances. In both cases, there is an expectation of regular denominational collective worship, which will contribute to the distinctively Christian ethos of the institution.

In either case, church schools offer an opportunity to model a eucharistic community among the youngest members of society, for the benefit of the wider world in which such schools are set. Church schools, because their ethos can reflect the ethos of the faith community that helps support them, represent an opportunity for the Church to model community and show what it means to live in the new creation. This is especially significant nowadays, since far more people will be made familiar with the Christian narrative of salvation history through schooling than through participation in the formal structures of the Church. It is estimated, for example, that 900,000 young people are enrolled in Church of England primary and secondary schools. In comparison, fewer than 200,000 people of the same age group regularly attend church services.[14]

---

13 Smith, Alan, 2008, *God-Shaped Mission*, Norwich: Canterbury Press, p. 84.

14 House of Bishops, *The Way Ahead*, p. 10.

The proliferation of church schools in rural areas presents a unique opportunity to form a community that lives by the Church's narrative of salvation history and serves the needs of the wider community. Through direct involvement in voluntary aided and voluntary controlled schools, the rural church can not only help the school build community generally; it can help the school to model a particular kind of community, founded on eucharistic values, and in which Christ's love and justice are known and shared. For this reason I believe that *Faith in the Countryside* was right to recommend that serious thought be given to the appointment of clergy to posts involving responsibility for a rural church school.[15] If clergy do not take the opportunity to become fully involved in the life of a church school in the area in which they minister, then they are missing one of the biggest opportunities to contribute to the life of the community. Thus, it should be a requirement of appointment to such posts that clergy have a demonstrable commitment to, and enthusiasm for, working constructively with schools. Even in the general case, if a rural clergyperson does not want to work with schools, then one would have to wonder how well suited he or she is to ministry in the countryside, where engagement by young people in the life of the community is a major challenge that the Church is uniquely placed to address.

Similarly, staff appointments, and the appointment of head-teachers in particular, should reflect the commitment of the Church of England to close working with its schools. A head-teacher with only a nominal commitment to a life of faith would seem to be an unwise appointment to a rural church school, given the profound opportunity such a school offers for Christ-like modelling of community. Prospective headteachers should make clear that they wish the school to bear the distinctive marks

---

15 ACORA, *Faith in the Countryside*, p. 217.

of the Christian community, in order that it can properly embody the values by which it has been constituted. They should make a commitment to close working with the local parish church, and be asked at interview about ways in which they could envisage implementing this. Alongside assessment of the talents and abilities of applicants as educators, and their skills as administrators and managers, their vision for the community of faith that a good church school can become ought to be central to selection processes.

Where governors are appointed in order to reflect a school's Christian ethos, it is important for the Church to recognize that, for some members, this may be a vocation to which they are particularly called. In the same way that the Church works hard to foster vocations to licensed and ordained ministry, it should have structures at parish level in order to encourage the exploration of vocations to involvement in local schooling. In a voluntary controlled school in particular, where the Church only appoints a minority of governors, it is especially important for the Church's appointed governors to have a vision for Christian education and a strong sense of calling to their role. Apathy will be of little use to anyone involved in the school's life, and its prevalence among governing bodies could lead to the nullification of the distinctive opportunity offered to rural communities by virtue of having a church school in their midst. If the Church has a commitment to its schools, such a commitment needs to be honoured in the Church's selection of governors at the local level.

A vision for rural church schools

Is there a vision for rural church schools? I suspect it is sufficient to say in response to this question that many of the hallmarks of a good church school are also the hallmarks of the Church itself. So rural church schools can be at the centre of their communities alongside the churches that support them, furthering opportunities for building community and offering education for all God's people. Rural churches might offer adult education in the form of discipleship courses, for example, which are delivered in church school premises and advertised through the school's network of parents. Or rural churches might take responsibility for managing fundraising on behalf of their schools, say, by forming a league of friends. The church might hold some of its social events in school grounds, or offer acts of worship that are centred on the school rather than the church. In all these ways, the community can be invited to share in the ownership of a rural school, and be drawn into its life, thereby also being drawn into the life of community modelled by the Church.

More particularly, I would urge rural churches to take their involvement in the worshipping life of church schools especially seriously. Both voluntary controlled and voluntary aided schools have denominational worship enshrined in their policies: church members should be encouraged to draw up rotas of worship leaders, and plan acts of worship that will truly bring the staff and pupils of their schools into God's presence. One of the themes of this book has been the transforming power of Christian worship: when churches have the opportunity to share this among the wider community, it should be grasped with thanks and praise. What is more, the route from school to Church should be made as straightforward as possible, so that those who encounter the Church through its work with church schools might more readily participate in its worshipping life. This involves rural church members working hard to exercise a ministry of welcome to parents, pupils and church school staff, in order that they feel included in the worshipping community, and encouraged to come into the way of discipleship.

Rural church schools might well be the lifeblood of rural communities, representing as they do an aspect of the Church that is less threatening, and less likely to polarize opinion, than the

Church itself. By working constructively through its schools, the rural church can help build community in ways that share Christ's love and justice with the wider community, without running the risk – ever present in relation to church activities – of putting people off. That does not mean that church schools represent an opportunity for the rural church to undertake mission by stealth; rather, it reflects the idea that schools can be important contributors to the flourishing of rural communities, and that church schools in particular should view this as a part of their institutional identity. If the Church works effectively through its schools in the countryside, it can live its Eucharist in new and exciting ways, for the good of the world.

A brief survey of rural services

The rural population grew by 800,000 in the years between 1998 and 2008, and the Office of National Statistics predicts that the overall number of people living in the countryside will have grown by a further 16 per cent by 2028. This puts substantial pressure on rural services, but the government remains committed to its policy of maintaining essential services wherever possible.[16] The commonly rehearsed idea that rural services are under significant threat is therefore something of a red herring: as it happens, service provision in some areas has expanded over the past decade, and this has often happened at a more rapid rate than in urban areas. Even post offices, a much publicized victim of Whitehall's cutbacks, have closed with far less frequency in rural areas than in towns and cities, meaning that the idea of a public-sector industry delivering services at the point of need rather than demand remains more or less intact. Almost half of all the UK's post offices are located in rural areas, which could

16 DETRA 2000, *Our Countryside: The Future,* London: The Stationery Office, p. 6.

91

seem like a disproportionate allocation when we remember that 80 per cent of the population lives in urban areas. This does not account for the fact that the rural population is more thinly spread, however, and it is certainly the case that many village communities have been badly affected by the loss of post offices and shops.

Considered as a whole, 15 per cent of service outlets for the industries considered in the *State of the Countryside* report are located in rural areas (the report follows the Office of National Statistics in defining 'rural' as areas with populations of fewer than 10,000).[17] This includes 35 per cent of all petrol stations, 30 per cent of primary schools, and 34 per cent of the country's pubs and restaurants. In each of these cases, the government made a commitment in 2000 to safeguarding their place in rural communities, because of the enhancement to quality of life that each was thought to bring. One of the few services to have dropped away substantially in rural areas is Job Centres, and this has coincided with a rise in internet access, facilitating online job searches by rural inhabitants.

Supermarkets have a growing presence in rural communities, with the number of outlets rising by 4 per cent in 2007 alone. Given that, in the same year, the average rural dweller travelled 4 km to their nearest supermarket, this upward trend might be seen as a positive step in terms of convenience for shoppers and the overall reduction of carbon emissions. But the arrival of supermarket outlets in rural areas reduces the opportunities for small businesses selling local produce: when there is no supermarket, such shops can compete with the multiples on convenience if not on price. When there is a supermarket on their own patch, they will lose on both counts – and even the appeal of food traceability is likely to be insufficient to train shoppers out of their supermarket purchasing habits, especially as the multiples

---

17 CRC, 2008, *State of the Countryside*, p. 7.

are themselves working hard to be open about the origins of their products. The Church can be countercultural here, of course, by encouraging members to eat seasonal and locally sourced produce via the means I described at the end of Chapter 4. Either way, analysis of this trend reminds us that increased provision of rural service outlets is not always the best thing for rural communities. It depends upon the service being offered, and whether it furthers or diminishes our relationships with one another, and with the rest of creation.

How can the Church protect rural services?

Notwithstanding the supermarket example, which is something of an exception, my argument is that vibrant rural services can play a role in building community. Since the rural church has a commitment to the flourishing of its local communities, its members should seek to make use of rural services, and encourage others to do likewise. One of the biggest reasons rural services disappear is because they are small businesses, and businesses depend upon continued custom for their survival. Rural pubs and village shops are good examples of services that rural dwellers claim to prize, but of which they often make insufficient use to safeguard their future. It might seem like one of the less burdensome requirements of a life of faith to make sure one pays regular visits to one's local pub, but it is a fine way of aiding the vibrancy of one's community. Moreover, the decision to give as much business as possible to one's local post office might seem fairly insignificant – but it can make the difference between the continued survival of that business and its disappearance. Theologians do not need to be economists to appreciate the basic insight that if rural dwellers do not make frequent use of the services they claim to value, they are poorly positioned to complain when those services disappear.

To this end, the rural church should think seriously about ways in which it can encourage use of rural services by members of its communities. It could, for example, hold regular quiz nights in the village pub, raising money for charity and bringing custom to the bar at the same time. Alternatively, a free parish magazine could be given to every person who spends more than five pounds a week in the village shop or post office, thereby encouraging people to use their local facility and keep in touch with the community's news. In both of these examples, the church undertakes something that is profoundly theological, despite its pragmatic texture: it finds creative ways of building community, which bear the distinctive hallmarks of life in the new creation.

It needs recognizing, however, that there are some services that cannot be sustained merely through regular use. GP surgeries are slightly rarer in the countryside now than they were ten years ago, despite some £100 million being spent on health provision in rural areas in the same period. The problem has nothing to do with a lack of demand for doctors in the countryside. The difficulty is that rural surgeries tend to be one-doctor practices. If that person retires, or relocates, or leaves the profession, it may herald the closure of a surgery serving hundreds of residents. As with many professions, doctors choosing to work in general practice in rural areas might not achieve much status professionally, or feel as if they are making full use of their skills, which can make it difficult to recruit into such roles.

Rural theology reminds us that our imaging of the trinitarian God involves a commitment to the good of the other. When it comes to the Church's response to the issues that arise when a rural community loses its doctor, such a concern might be made manifest in a project to help transport residents to the nearest surgery. This might involve the purchase of a minibus, say, and the part-time employment of a driver. But if the Church is serious in its commitment to be other-facing, such expenses should not seem insurmountable. A fundraising campaign might enable the community to work together in resourcing a project like this; local businesses might be encouraged to contribute in some way; and the Church should ultimately be willing to redirect its own funds in supporting such a scheme. The Eucharist shows us how to be friends, and trains us out of selfish ways: if use of church resources for the good of community members whose lives are negatively affected by withdrawal of key services has to be traded against the Church's non-essential internal projects, then it should seem like no sacrifice at all.

A development of the idea that the rural church should see its imaging of the trinitarian God expressed in practical support for people who struggle to cope with the loss of a key service from their community is the idea that the Church can itself become a rural service-provider. This has been seen most readily in the post office example, where rural churches have taken over village post offices and run them on a not-for-profit basis from church buildings. The Revd Peter Cunliffe was the first vicar in England to be appointed a village sub-postmaster, after the parish of Hemingford Grey in the diocese of Ely took over the running of the local post office when its former owner retired.[18] The initiative has since received formal support from the Archbishops' Council, and is seen by the government as a way of compensating rural communities for the loss of post offices arising from nationwide rationalization. The pastoral opportunities it presents are manifold, since the Church will come into contact with a far greater proportion of the community than it would expect to see in Sunday worship. It also provides a means for the Church to share Christ's love and justice with the communities of which it is a part, for the decision to serve a rural community in this way is a powerful witness to the unselfish life of discipleship in which Christians are formed through participation in the Eucharist.

---

18 http://www.cofe.anglican.org/info/yearreview/jun07/postoffices.html (accessed March 2010).

Rural theology requires the Church to take an interest in rural services because they contribute to the building of vibrant communities. The Church should therefore be an advocate for the community when service provision is threatened, or when the arrival of new services looks set to threaten the relationship between humans, and between humans and the rest of creation. What is more, when services disappear from rural communities, the Church should see itself as having an important role in ameliorating the negative implications of the loss of services, even if that involves directing its own resources away from non-essential internal projects in order to serve the community. And, s a continuation of that idea, I believe the Church should look seriously at providing rural services such as post offices when they are not available from any other source in the local community.

As with its involvement in schools, the rural church can be a Eucharist for the good of its local communities through the interest of its members in rural services. Church members, by discerning those services that help build rural community, can actively support them – individually and corporately – and thereby contribute to the flourishing of communities that reflect God's purposes for creation. And it might not need saying that such action by church members could well be habitual, as it is performed by those who have been formed through participation in the Eucharist to take their part in the drama of salvation history. The rural church's practical involvement in these aspects of the life of its local communities is a living witness to its own eucharistic life; it is a means by which Christ's love and justice can be shared among those who live in the countryside.

6

The Rural Landscape and Leisure

This chapter is concerned with the ways in which humans interact with the rural landscape in their leisure time. It is thus primarily concerned with the relation between humans and the rest of creation. I suggest that spending time in the countryside enables us to connect with the non-human world in profound ways, to place ourselves in a larger scheme of existence, and that it provides an opportunity for spiritual growth. For these reasons, I want to describe opportunities to spend time in the countryside as sacramental. I argue that we must take the right things for granted in our interaction with the rural landscape. At the heart of this discussion is my assertion that rural theology requires us to have a right relationship with the rest of creation, as well as with one another. Finally, I consider briefly how this relationship can be honoured by rural church members, who are formed through their eucharistic practice to share Christ's love and justice with the world, with particular reference to the care of churchyards.

The call of the wild

It starts with beauty. Speaking personally, my encounter with the rural environment is mediated principally through my experience of its profound beauty. To give an example, there is a solitary silver birch tree that stands about 100 yards from my study window. It is the first thing I see when I glance up from my desk in search of lost words or phrases. As I write, its branches are more or less bare, just budding, as spring begins to warm the ground. The bark is a mix of shining white and scuffed black, in the way of silver birches; its trunk surprisingly yielding to the breezes that blow through the valley and bend it this way and that. If I did not have a book to write, I would spend many hours simply watching the tree and letting my mind roam free. I would forget for a moment my worldly concerns; I would allow my brain to freewheel, noting nothing apart from the comings and goings of birds from the orchard between my house and the tree, and the occasional mewing of sheep in the field beyond. But I would be formed through such an encounter with the world beyond my study window; I would come to see something of the wonder of God's creation; and perhaps, viewing it through the eyes of one who is formed through participation in the Eucharist, I might begin to better understand my place in the new creation. So it starts with beauty, and it ends with God's redeeming action in the world.

Such is my interaction with the natural world immediately outside my window. It is only a partial telling of a theological story concerning human interactions with nature, but many of its features obtain in relation to all human encounters with the rest of creation, whether they are told by theologians or otherwise. There are common features to such stories, and they relate to the responses that are shared by human beings who put themselves in the way of God's creation by spending time in the countryside in contemplation and leisure. I suggest that there are three broad things that we can say about spending time in the countryside in this way:

- it enables us to connect with the non-human world in profound ways;
- it enables us to place ourselves in a larger scheme of existence; and

- as a result of these two things, it provides an opportunity for spiritual growth.

I shall now consider each of these things in turn.

Spending time in the countryside enables us to connect with the non-human world in profound ways

The landscape essayist and Cambridge Fellow Robert Macfarlane begins his exploration of the idea of the wild, in *The Wild Places*, with a sequence in which he describes climbing a beech tree on the edge of Cambridge where he lives. Macfarlane is a poetic and thoughtful writer whose work captures the beauty of the natural world, and who also writes eloquently about the impact of the non-human creation on human beings. His book, which describes his quest to find places of genuine wilderness in twenty-first-century Britain and Ireland, reminds us of an important issue in relation to human engagement with the natural world in this country. Macfarlane reminds us that much of our landscape is actually made by humans, produced as a result of agriculture or other forms of human intervention. Macfarlane recounts his struggles to find places that have not been influenced by the activities of humans, and might therefore deserve the moniker of 'wildness'. He manages to find just a few such places, and his book is tinged with regret about their scarcity.[1]

The difficulty of Macfarlane's search might lead us to assume that the idea that spending time in the countryside can somehow connect us to the non-human world is wrongheaded. If, after all, our countryside is basically made by human beings, then it is surely an unlikely arena in which to experience the non-human world with any degree of profundity. But such an assumption

---

1 Macfarlane, Robert, 2007, *The Wild Places*, London: Granta Books, p. 9.

misses the very real presence of non-human creatures in our countryside. Even if the idea that the countryside is 'wild' is mistaken, that does not detract from its status as a place of encounter between different species. A walk in the countryside raises the possibility of crossing paths with, to name but a few, farm animals, birds, deer, plants and trees. If we go there in the hope of experiencing God's unfettered creation – untouched, so to say, by human hand – then we will be disappointed. But if we go in the hope of encountering other creatures, plants and trees, then we stand a high chance of being rewarded.

Macfarlane recognizes this himself while reflecting upon his tree-climbing. Although just a mile away from the fringes of the city, his tree is a place in which he comes into close contact with other species. He describes how, if he remains still for long enough, birds return to the tree around him and go about their doings: 'Blackbirds fussing in the leaf litter; wrens [whirring] from twig to twig so quickly they seem to teleport; once a grey partridge, venturing anxiously from cover.'[2] Although Macfarlane's story is primarily concerned with his attempt to connect with the natural world in wild places, his account of his beech tree in Cambridge is a reminder to us that, when humans and other species come into contact in an environment influenced by humans, there can be profound connections between them. Such an insight is of particular significance to the theological story I am telling in this book.

I argued in Chapter 4 that rearing livestock can provide a means of furthering relationships between species. In this chapter, I suggest that a way in which humans find their place in the new creation is through encountering other species, and deepening their relation with the non-human world. A landscape that has been formed by human hands need not undermine such deepening of relationships. Indeed, just because our rural landscape

---

2 Macfarlane, *The Wild Places*, p. 4.

has been influenced by human activity, it is a place where there is a history of interaction between the species. Such interaction is spoken of with great wit in Andy Merrifield's compelling book, *The Wisdom of Donkeys*. Merrifield is a disillusioned academic, who escapes the pressurized world of the Research Assessment Exercise and sets up home in the Auvergne, in France. He embarks upon an extended walk with a borrowed donkey, Gribouille, which is reminiscent of Robert Louis Stevenson's famous adventure with a grey donkey called Modestine, in his *Travels with a Donkey in the Cevennes* (1878). Merrifield's book is an erudite read, reminding its readers of the significance of time spent outdoors to human well-being and wholeness. More importantly for our purposes, it is a litany of the connections that can be made between humans and non-humans when they spend time in one another's company. Merrifield writes:

> There's something amazing about watching donkeys graze in the middle of nowhere. It's a kind of therapy, even a sort of meditation. You can both lose and find yourself. An Australian proverb says that when you watch donkeys in a meadow, don't forget your chair. You can observe them for hours on end – it's hypnotic and addictive. It's hard to drag yourself away once you're smitten.[3]

And so it continues, with Merrifield offering countless such passages in which we are transported to the French countryside and invited imaginatively to participate in his burgeoning relationship with Gribouille and the other creatures he encounters on his journey. The book is no ordinary travelogue; rather, it is a serious philosophical and spiritual engagement with the experience of spending time in the company of non-human species and adjusting one's

---

3 Merrifield, Andy, 2008, *The Wisdom of Donkeys*, London: Short Books, p. 8.

ways as a result. Merrifield emerges from his experience with a greater self-understanding, uniquely born out of his encounter with another creature. 'In Gribouille's presence,' he states, 'my whole life has passed before me. He's given me a chance, perhaps a second . . . to analyse it . . . to go on living . . . to anoint it all . . . with the healing balm of hope, with the creative powers of imagination.'[4] Gribouille has become a friend, a companion, with whom Merrifield feels a creaturely connection that he would not have experienced were it not for their coming into one another's presence.

Spending time in the countryside, where we can encounter the non-human creation and give ourselves time to come to understand it, enables a profound connection to be experienced between humans and the rest of God's good world. It is thus a sacramental moment to be in the countryside in this way, to experience God's creative presence through encounter with his creatures. The rural church should seek to encourage such moments, and to facilitate their occurrence.

Spending time in the countryside enables us to place ourselves in a larger scheme of existence

As well as enhanced connectedness to the non-human world, spending time in the countryside provides us with a sense of perspective; it enables us to identify ourselves as part of a larger creation, through which God's purposes are played out, and in which we participate as those who are called to image the trinitarian God who creates, reconciles and saves the world. When I say that the moments I have been talking about in this chapter, of humans spending time in the countryside and encountering other species, are sacramental, I am identifying their similarity to the Eucharist. In this act of worship, we come into the risen Christ's presence

---

4 Merrifield, *Wisdom of Donkeys*, p. 243.

and are transformed as those who belong to the new creation, are shown how to be friends, are trained out of selfishness and know that we are accepted because of our frailty. Participation in the Eucharist is one way in which we are able to place ourselves in a larger scheme of existence, recognizing that redemption is for the whole of creation and that being human involves taking our part alongside the other creatures in the drama of salvation history. Another way in which this can happen is through spending time in contemplation and leisure in the countryside. For it is here that, as a result of profound connections with the rest of creation, we come to see that we are part of a whole. We see that non-human species are part of God's good creation, fallen, and reconciled to God through Christ's saving work. We come to see that we participate in the drama of salvation history as those who are called to image God, who has created everything. By staring the rest of creation in the face, so to say, we are reminded of our place within it.

I think it is this sense of coming to know one's place in a larger scheme of existence that another great landscape essayist, Adam Nicholson, writes about in his *Sea Room*. The volume is a story of Nicholson's encounter with the Shiants, three islands off the coast of Scotland, which his father gave him, when he turned 18. Nicholson recounts the many occasions when he has spent time on the islands, and gained a sense of perspective about his life and his place in the world. In one memorable moment, Nicholson describes collecting water from a spring on one of the islands, using a shallow bowl to gather the liquid from the surface of the earth, where it bubbles through rocks to form a pool. His description of this process demonstrates how our encounter with the non-human world has the power to show us our part in a deeper narrative of existence. Nicholson writes:

> The gathering of the Shiants' sweet water . . . always feels to me like an engagement with one of the oldest layers of the place. Where the materials like this are constant, and the uses

103

to which they are put will always be the same whatever your beliefs, or language, or habit of mind, history collapses. It is as if time has not passed. This delicate sipping at an island spring is the same now as it must always have been . . . This is not, as people so often say of a landscape, a manuscript on which the past has been written and erased over and over again. It is a place in which many different times coexist, flowing at different speeds, enshrining different worlds.[5]

Whatever our beliefs about the world, Nicholson seems to be saying, we come to recognize our place within it when we connect to its non-human constituents. This is one of the most important things we can say about our interaction with the rural landscape, since it reminds us that such time is not mere rest and relaxation. For Christians, it reminds us that spending this time is part of our coming to know ourselves as creatures of a good God, who take our place in the drama of salvation history. It is leisure time in the truest sense of the word, meaning that it is formational, and capable of deepening our relation to God and to the rest of creation. That is why I am suggesting that spending this time in the countryside can be sacramental – more than that, that it is similar to our participation in the Eucharist – because it forms us as those who recognize that we are part of a bigger story, that we belong to a bigger creation.

Spending time in the countryside provides an opportunity for spiritual growth

It hardly needs saying, given the two other things I have already said about spending time in the countryside, that it is a spiritual experience, and that it is therefore an opportunity for spiritual

---

5 Nicholson, Adam, 2001, *Sea Room*, London: HarperCollins, p. 109.

growth. There is, of course, a long history of Christian disciples who seek a deeper spirituality by spending time in the natural world. The *peregrini*, or Christian pilgrims, of whom Macfarlane writes in *The Wild Places* and whose journeys he sometimes chooses to follow, deliberately sought places where they could spend time in contemplation of the non-human world in order to deepen their relationship with God.[6] The idea that contemplation of the natural world can deepen our relation with God is hardly new, as we are reminded by Jesus' own time in the wilderness (Matt. 4; Mark 1.12ff.; Luke 4) and by the example of Christian saints such as St Patrick. Even those unfamiliar with the tradition of spiritual formation through encounter with nature that is associated with some of the best parts of the Celtic tradition would surely resonate with the idea that spending time in rural surroundings provides an opportunity for spiritual growth. Few people can have experienced the sense of connection with the non-human world, and the discernment of one's place in a wider scheme of existence that comes from such time, without also experiencing it as a spiritual moment. When we put ourselves in the way of God's creation, we are undertaking an activity such as we undertake in the Eucharist, by opening ourselves up to the good things that God has done, giving thanks for his gifts, and celebrating our reconciliation to God in the new creation. Rural theology has a particular interest in the ways in which humans interact with the rural landscape for precisely this reason: if such interaction is an opportunity for spiritual growth, as I am arguing, then it is something that the rural church, through its eucharistic presence in the countryside, should seek to support, and provide further opportunities for people to undertake.

---

6 Macfarlane, *The Wild Places*, p. 24.

Remembering our place in creation

I have stated throughout this work that rural theology is concerned that humans have a right relationship with the rest of creation, and with one another. When it comes to our interaction with the rural landscape, the importance of our relation to the non-human world is paramount. It can be very easy to assume that the natural world is only of value in so far as it contributes to our leisure activities and enjoyment. But, as my discussion in the previous section indicates, our interaction with the rural environment demonstrates that spending leisure time in the countryside can be about far more than merely unwinding from the pressures of everyday life. It can be a profoundly spiritual experience, a contemplative time, and therefore leisure in the truest sense of the term, in which we are connected to the non-human world and through which we are able to place ourselves in a larger scheme of existence. I am making two interrelated points here: on the one hand, we must approach our encounter with the rural landscape in an appropriate way (that is, one in which we are concerned that we have a right relationship with the rest of creation), and that, on the other hand, we realize the precise nature of our relationship with the non-human world as a result of our spiritual encounter with it, which can be facilitated by spending leisure time in the countryside.

There will always be a risk that, when it comes to human use of rural areas for leisure purposes, we abuse the natural world and try to mould it to our own ends. I have established that farming – the archetypal interaction between humans and the natural world – can be a way of furthering the relationships between species when it is done responsibly and on a relatively small scale. In other words, farming can be a means through which humans are enabled to have a right relationship with the non-human world, and thereby image the trinitarian God in ways that we come to take for granted through participation in the Eucharist.

Similarly, when appropriate care is taken over our use of the rural landscape for leisure activities, it can provide an opportunity, like farming, for furthering the interaction between the human and the non-human elements of God's creation.

Since the implementation of the Countryside and Rights of Way Act 2000, the British public has gained access to a further 566,300 hectares of mountain, moor, heath and down, and 369,000 hectares of common land.[7] It is no surprise to learn that use of the countryside for leisure activities has burgeoned in this time, with walking, angling and game-shooting enjoying particular popularity. In each case, there is a risk that human interests ride roughshod over the interests of the rest of creation, and that the opportunities for spiritual growth that such activities offer are missed, because they are made subservient to the consequentialist good of human pleasure or satisfaction. That is why it is important for the Church to embody its Eucharist for the good of the world around it. The Church tells a story that reminds humans of their proper place in the new creation; it is a story that must inform our thinking about the ways in which we interact with the rural landscape, and about the ways in which we therefore implicitly value the natural world.

John Oliver reminds us of three important principles that arose from the Lambeth Conference of 1998. They are:

1. The divine spirit is sacramentally present in creation, which itself ought to be treated with reverence, respect and gratitude.
2. Human beings are both co-partners with the rest of creation and living bridges between heaven and earth, with responsibility to make personal and corporate sacrifices for the common good of all creation.

---

7 CRC, *State of the Countryside*, p. 128.

3. The redemptive purposes of God in Jesus Christ extend to the whole of creation.[8]

Oliver regards these principles as central to our thinking about human interaction with the rest of creation, since they remind us of our place in the created order as those who are made in God's image and who must therefore take appropriate care of the world around them.[9] Therefore, when making decisions about our interaction with the rural landscape for the purposes of leisure, it is important that these principles, which lie at the heart of rural theology, are properly enshrined in our conduct. But we can say even more than that, because when the appropriate conditions are in place for human interaction with the rural landscape, an enhanced awareness of the truth of these principles can be expected, rather in the manner of our participation in the Eucharist. The Church has a twofold responsibility, then. First, it should ensure that human interaction with the rural landscape helps further a right relationship with the rest of creation. Second, it should provide opportunities for spiritual encounter with the non-human world, rather than seeing rural leisure valued only because it helps humans unwind or brings them pleasure.

When it comes to the first part of its responsibility to the rural communities of which it is a part, the Church does well to remember that the natural world is to be valued appropriately. So as to image the trinitarian God to whom we are reconciled through Christ's saving work, we must acknowledge that this work is undertaken for the whole of creation, not just humans. As I argued in Chapter 1, creation is not merely the backdrop against which the drama of salvation history is played out; it is a

---

8 Lambeth Conference, 1999, *Official Report of the Lambeth Conference 1998*, Pennsylvania: Morehouse Publishing, p. 379.

9 Oliver, John, 2004, 'Biodiversity', in Jeremy Martineau, Leslie Francis and Peter Francis (eds), *Changing Rural Life*, Norwich: Canterbury Press, p. 119.

part of the story. This means that the natural world has intrinsic, rather than merely instrumental, worth. It means that we ought to take the interests of the non-human world into account just as much as our own interests when deciding how to use our leisure time. Activities that can cause destruction and harm to the environment ought to be avoided, therefore, even if they produce a great deal of pleasure for their human participants. Moreover, the Church might have a role in encouraging the use of the rural landscape for other activities that can help deepen relationships between the species, and even in providing opportunities for such a deepening.

Whether such activities are destructive to the relationship between human and non-human species can be difficult to discern. John Oliver points out, for example, that hunting could well be a way of furthering the relationship, since it encourages biodiversity and therefore aids the flourishing of the landscape.[10] Southgate also suggests that hunting might, like farming (as I discussed in Chapter 4), be a means of 'forming a pattern of community between humans and the non-human creation' that we do well to preserve.[11] It is certainly true that when the breeding and rearing of birds is conducted with appropriate care, pheasant shooting, for instance, can be extremely good for the ecosystem in which it takes place. A study currently being undertaken by a PhD student at the University of Bristol is investigating ways in which to enhance best practice in the management of land for game-hunting, in order that biodiversity is maintained while balancing the commercial interests of landowners and gamekeepers.[12] The project recognizes

---

10 Oliver, 'Biodiversity', p. 131.

11 Southgate, Christopher, 2008, *The Groaning of Creation*, Louisville: Westminster John Knox Press, p. 121.

12 Davey, Catherine, 2010, 'The Impact of Game Management for Pheasant Shooting on the Biodiversity of Agricultural Ecosystems', project description available at: http://www.bio.bris.ac.uk/research/mammal/pheasants.html (accessed March 2010).

the quality of relationship between humans and non-humans in the breeding and rearing of birds for shooting, and is seeking to advance this relationship for the benefit of all. Despite its consequentialist tenor, the project might be a helpful means of exploring the nature of the relation between hunter and hunted, when hunting is seen as akin to farming – that is, the humane breeding, rearing and killing of animals for human consumption. Theologians would want to tell a different story about the reasons for making sure this relationship is a right relationship: because it is a part of the participation of all God's creatures in the new creation, rather than because it is a way of producing desirable outcomes, such as wealthier landowners or healthier birds. As with the farming example, where I argued that small-scale mixed farms are an opportunity to ensure that humans have a right relationship with the rest of creation, if appropriate techniques are employed, certain forms of hunting might well have a place in a rural theology that seeks a deepening of relationships between species. Perhaps more importantly, other forms of hunting, which are destructive to the environment and represent the causing of terror by humans to other creatures for the sake of sport, with no notion that the kill will be eaten, and without a relationship with its human counterparts prior to being hunted, should certainly have no place in a Christian story about rural life.

The rural church and leisure

I have been arguing that putting ourselves in the way of God's creation for the purposes of leisure is different from using the countryside as a context in which to participate in our favourite hobbies and pastimes. It involves an intentional interaction with the rural landscape that leaves one open to a genuine encounter with the non-human world. In a survey undertaken in 2007, 17 per cent of people claimed to have taken a walk in the countryside in the previous month.[13] Walking is a clear example of a rural pursuit that provides an opportunity for genuine encounter with the natural world; as is fishing, in which approximately 20 per cent of the population participates.[14] In both cases, humans come into the presence of the non-human world peacefully and respectfully. They can be still in the way of Macfarlane in his beech tree, meaning that wildlife is undisturbed, and perhaps even comes close to the human visitors in its midst. When undertaken reverentially and with the right attitude, activities such as this can be encouraged, and even facilitated, by the Church. The rural church might have a role in providing a vision to rural walkers and anglers of what their time in the countryside can bring (a sense of connection with the non-human world, a placing of oneself in a larger scheme of existence, and an opportunity for spiritual growth). Greater education about species variety, for example, or about the workings of the natural world, might help to generate enthusiasm and increased knowledge among people who would otherwise only see the rural landscape as a backdrop for their leisure activities. This knowledge can then facilitate a genuine coming into community with the non-human world, which might not otherwise take place. So, for instance, the rural church might position information boards in its car parks, or outside its gates, which give information about the species likely to be encountered in the locality, and share something of the theological understanding of creation that I have been exploring here and elsewhere in this book. This need not be done in a hectoring or overly evangelistic tone; but if visitors to the rural landscape come to share in our understanding of it as part of God's good creation, with which we are required to have a right relationship, then it seems to me that the rural church can be a genuinely eucharistic presence in the countryside.

---

13 CRC, *State of the Countryside*, p. 132.
14 CRC, *State of the Countryside*, p. 132.

Of course, the use of the rural landscape for leisure activities can lead to conflicts in the countryside, as David Walker observes.[15] The interests of those who spend time in the countryside primarily for reasons of leisure can come into conflict with the interests of those who live and work there. Footpaths that pass directly in front of private houses can cause anxiety among homeowners who wish to preserve their privacy. The use of public spaces for car parking can ruin the peace and tranquillity of a village setting, as can an influx of visitors. Farmers can find that their work is interfered with by walkers and anglers who want access to their land. Set against this is the contribution made to the rural economy by the use of the countryside for leisure activities, which is estimated to be around £9 billion. There is inevitably ambivalence among rural dwellers when it comes to the use of their local areas for leisure activities, and the Church can often end up trying to mediate between conflicting interests.

Wherever possible, it seems to me that the Church's eucharistic presence in a rural community requires that it encourage the use of the landscape for appropriate leisure activities while limiting the disruption caused to rural residents and workers. Clearly, if farmers cannot open their fields to walkers because it will damage crops, the Church should understand their position and not seek to undermine it. But the theological story I am trying to tell in this volume about the countryside necessarily recognizes the significance of leisure. It is an opportunity for spiritual growth and well-being, for wholeness, that we are reminded of by the Sabbath rest taken by the creator God on the seventh day (Gen. 2.3).

The Sabbath is the climax of the creation narrative, and the bishops at the 1998 Lambeth Conference invested it with especial meaning in relation to our interaction with the non-human world. As Oliver notes, they called for a reinvigoration of the

---

15 Walker, David S., 2004, 'Private Property and Public Good', in Martineau, Francis and Francis (eds), *Changing Rural Life*, pp. 79–98.

Sabbath, 'not as a nostalgic symbol of a religious past, but as a feast of redemption and anticipation of the ecological harmony and sustainable equilibrium of Christ's Kingdom'.[16] The Sabbath is at the heart of the new creation; its loss might even be taken as a sign of our fallen state. If the Church has a story to tell about human interaction with the rural landscape, it is that the Sabbath provides an opportunity for disciples to place themselves in the drama of salvation history by deepening their relationship with the non-human world and coming to recognize its intrinsic worth. The Church therefore has a role in facilitating those leisure activities, like walking, nature watching, and perhaps even fishing and certain types of hunting, which enable such a deepening relationship. Moreover, the rural church can provide particular opportunities for this type of rural leisure through effective management of its churchyards.

Rural churchyards – places of life

Ten years after *Faith in the Countryside* was published, a much shorter document was issued by the Arthur Rank Centre which sought to identify ways in which the advice of the Archbishops' Commission had been acted upon by rural churches. *Celebrating the Rural Church* was a hopeful publication, which showed how the rural church had taken at least some of the practical recommendations included in *Faith in the Countryside* to heart. The report also identified future challenges and changes to the rural scene that had occurred in the intervening decade. One of the most exciting elements of the updated report is its recognition that rural churchyards provide a significant opportunity to further the relationship between humans and the non-human creation; that rural churchyards can be places of life, thanksgiving

---

16 Lambeth Conference, *Official Report*, p. 92; see also Oliver, 'Biodiversity', p. 121.

and praise, as well as places in which the dead are laid to rest. Thus, the report states: 'Every church building surrounded by a churchyard potentially has a tailor-made site where conservationists can demonstrate what is possible for the promotion of conservation and the enhancement of the natural environment.'[17]

More than this, churchyards can be places where people are encouraged to come and spend time in contemplation of God's good creation. It seems to me that the grounds of church buildings, in which we are called to give thanks and praise for God's gifts to his creation, are the best possible places to which we can go in order to deepen our relationship with the non-human world. Reminded as we are in churchyards of the saints who have gone before us, we are connected to the new creation in Christ in profound ways. We might well come to see our place in a larger scheme of existence by virtue of seeing life among the resting places of the faithful departed; signs of hope that God's redemption is for all, that God will be all in all, and that we have been promised a place in his kingdom.

If rural leisure can be sacramental, when it involves putting ourselves in the way of God's creation, then the rural church might take special care that its churchyards are places of contemplation and genuine leisure. Admittedly, it might seem strange to some people that they should spend their free time among gravestones and reminders of human mortality. But if churchyards are places of life, where the natural world flourishes, where the beauty of creation is evidenced in celebration of the lives of the saints, where genuinely spiritual encounters between humans and other species can take place, then visiting churchyards for the purpose of deepening one's relationship with God, and with God's creation, would seem the most natural thing in the world to do. It would certainly seem a more natural way of remembering

---

17 Arthur Rank Centre, 2000, *Celebrating the Rural Church: 10 Years on from Faith in the Countryside*, Stoneleigh: ACORA Publishing, p. 37.

our dead than creating plastic-wrapped floral shrines that are out of kilter with the environment around them.

There is a wonderful little book by Nigel Cooper that advises church members about the best ways to manage churchyards in order to encourage wildlife and conserve a broad range of species. *Wildlife in Church and Churchyard* begins with a brief reflection on the potential for churchyards to be places in which humans come into right relationship with the rest of creation. Cooper states that our place in the new creation involves recognition of our mutuality with non-human species, and says that churchyards offer places in which we can 'catch this vision and act upon it'. That is to say, 'they can be places where we can practise living harmoniously with our fellow creatures, treasuring their presence among us. They can speak of how we see God's presence in creation and how we believe God wishes us to care for that creation.'[18]

Cooper's book is a practical guide to the management of churchyards, and I commend it to you. His suggestions provide a way in which rural church members can share Christ's love and justice with the world. By involving themselves in conservation of rural churchyards, church members can participate in a deepening of their relationship with the non-human creation. By welcoming to rural churchyards visitors who wish to put themselves in the way of God's creation, rural church members exercise the friendship and unselfishness that they are taught through their participation in the Eucharist. And, perhaps most fundamentally, they provide opportunities for sacramental moments in which people experience profound connections with the non-human world, are able to place themselves in a larger scheme of existence and, perhaps, have an opportunity for spiritual growth. Spending time in rural churchyards might seem like a peculiar

---

18 Cooper, Nigel, 2001, *Wildlife in Church and Churchyard*, 2nd edn, London: Church House Publishing, p. 1.

leisure pursuit, and, as I have suggested, there are certainly other ways in which humans can interact with the rural landscape in their leisure time that might prove just as formational. But taking appropriate care of churchyards in ways that encourage the flourishing of non-human species, and encouraging people to spend time in contemplation in them, is a way in which the rural church can serve the rural community. It is a way in which its members can image the trinitarian God. It is a way, in other words, in which the rural church can be a Eucharist for the world.

7

The Rural Church and the Eucharist

In this concluding chapter, I give some thought to the way the rural church lives the theological story of community. I argue that the rural church's members should see sharing Christ's love and justice with the world as a joyful activity. We are enabled through our participation in the Eucharist to take our place in the drama of salvation history. It is thus important that rural dwellers are encouraged to participate in the worshipping life of the Church. For this reason, I suggest that the rural church gives serious consideration to admitting children and people who have not been confirmed to the Eucharist. I also offer a somewhat briefer exploration of the idea of 'Communion by extension'. These issues seem to me to be especially important in rural areas, where the Church can be a key agent in community life. By opening its doors to the wider community, and loosening restrictions on the Eucharist that make it difficult for people in rural areas to participate in it, the rural church can help foster a community in which residents live for one another and for God. Or, to put it another way, by helping rural dwellers to image the trinitarian God, the Church in the countryside can be a Eucharist for the good of the world it is called to serve.

Why rural church attendance matters

The Prussian philosopher Immanuel Kant was probably right to say that the good will 'sparkles like a jewel',[1] although his

---

1 Kant, Immanuel, 1785, *The Foundations of the Metaphysic of Morals*, section one.

reasons for making such a claim differ from mine. Kant felt that moral motivation derived from the exercise of reason, meaning that people discerned how to act by reference to moral duties that were arrived at through abstract reflection. In contrast, I am arguing in this book that we come to act in certain ways because we are trained to do so, and that we get better at behaving well through practice. From a Christian perspective, this means that we become Christlike, that we become the sort of people who share Christ's love and justice with the world and come to put the good of other people ahead of our own interests. More fundamentally, I believe that, through Christ's saving work, we have been transformed, and that we come to image the trinitarian God through our participation in the Eucharist. In other words, we all have a place in the drama of salvation history, as those who are reconciled to God in the new creation. Participation in the Eucharist is a means of coming to discern our own place in that drama, by taking the right things for granted such that we act in Christlike ways as if by instinct.

Such an approach owes a great deal to the Aristotelian tradition in ethics. Aristotle believed that the way humans become good at anything is through practice. 'Anything that we have to learn to do,' he said, 'we learn by the doing of it: people become builders by building and instrumentalists by playing instruments.'[2] We might add to Aristotle's list by saying that people become good Christian disciples by being Christian disciples. That means that the way in which we come to take our place in the drama of salvation history is by participating in the life – and, in particular, in the eucharistic life – of the Church. It is by no means the case that there is no redemption outside the Church, since Christ's saving work is for all of creation. But it is true, I think, that we humans will struggle to discern our place in the drama of salvation history, or even to recognize

_____

2 Aristotle, 1953, *Ethics*, trans. J. A. K. Thomson, London: Penguin, p. 91.

the narrative by which we are shaped as God's creation, unless we are formed through our participation in the practices of the Church.

For this reason, it seems to matter whether people attend church or not. It matters not in terms of their salvation, for, as I have already said, Christ's life, death, resurrection and ascension initiated a new creation in which all are reconciled to God. But it matters because the way in which people will come to be fully human is through coming to discern their place in the drama of salvation history. Perhaps of more pertinence to my discussions in this book, it matters because the Church tells the best story about what it means to live in community. When rural churches are empty, we might well not expect to see flourishing communities around them.

Whichever way we look at it, church attendance in rural areas is at a historic low. A survey in 1998 showed that rural church attendance among Anglicans had dropped by an average of around 40 per cent since 1989.[3] While Alan Smith might be correct in asserting that the idea of a 'golden age when rural churches were full' is inaccurate,[4] it is nonetheless empirically verified that fewer rural inhabitants are now actively involved in the life of their local church than in previous generations.[5] By the lights of my argument, that means there are fewer people in rural areas who are familiar with the theological story about community, which I have said is the best one that can be told, capable of 'out-narrating' secular stories.

The suggestions I have made in Chapters 4–6 are predicated upon the assumption that church members have a distinctive

---

3 Arthur Rank Centre, 2004, 'Changes in Rural Church Statistics 1989–1998', Warwickshire: ARC, p. 3.

4 Smith, Alan, 2008, *God-Shaped Mission*, Norwich: Canterbury Press, p. 15.

5 Winter, M. and Short, C., 1993, 'Believing and Belonging: Religion in Rural England', *British Journal of Sociology*, vol. 44, pp. 635–51.

contribution to make to rural life. I have suggested that the rural church and its members:

- show friendship to farmers in order to reduce their feelings of isolation;
- help promote local produce, and make buying decisions that support small-scale mixed farmers;
- play a particular role in the life of local schools, and take special care to support particular local services;
- help ameliorate the negative effects of lost rural services by helping with transport, say, or even by providing some services – such as post offices – themselves;
- help facilitate the appropriate interaction of humans with the rural landscape, that churchyards can be places in which a sacramental deepening of relationships between humans and the rest of creation, and humans and other humans, can take place.

In each case, my assumption has been that the way in which rural church members live in the context of the countryside is informed through their participation in the Eucharist, as those who are called to share Christ's love and justice with the world.

If it turns out that the number of people participating in the rural church's worshipping life is dwindling, then my suggestions might be accused of being rather hopeful, to say the least. It matters that people are involved in the life of their local church, because it is in this way that they learn to take the right things for granted, and contribute to the flourishing of rural communities in some of the ways I have been describing. (As I stated in the Introduction, there are bound to be other ways of rural Christians contributing to community life; my ideas are merely suggestions for consideration.) That is not to say that the Church's influence in the countryside is limited by the size of its congregations. Rather, it is to emphasize the importance of the rural church welcoming people into its life, in order that they might come to discern the theological narrative by which the Church is constituted, and find their place within it.

Finding joy in being good

Part of the problem, it seems to me, is that the rural church can sometimes be a peculiarly joyless place. Christians have a regrettable habit of seeming to view exhaustion as virtuous, meaning that the more hollow-eyed church people become, the more effective they feel they are being as Christian disciples. It is a particular problem among clergy, but lay people are also prone to it. In the rural church, where there are often few people sharing the responsibility of maintaining the church's fabric, running services, visiting the sick and elderly and struggling to keep the church alive, this difficulty is especially pronounced. It often gives rural churches a rather unfriendly atmosphere, because church members are too worn out to bother with niceties. Of course, it is only right that we admire the commitment of those faithful disciples who keep the rural church alive; but we ought also to remind ourselves that the Christian life involves taking joy in one's participation in the coming kingdom.

Unless Christian disciples are joyful in their discipline of following Jesus, it seems unlikely that others will join in their walk. To put it another way, unless the rural church is a place of happiness and thanksgiving, its opportunity for helping to build rural community is curtailed. Through our participation in the Eucharist, we are shown how to be friends. It is important that our churches embody such friendship, and are places of warmth and welcome to would-be pilgrims. For, as John Thomson reminds us, unless those with whose lives the Church's ministry and mission intersects are encouraged to practise their faith in company with other Christian pilgrims, they will not be formed in the distinctive ways of discipleship.[6] In other words, the Church needs to attract new, and retain existing, members, or else there can be no hope that people will find their place in the drama of salvation history.

There is a very practical reason for rural church members to be joyful in their lives of discipleship. As we all know, it is much easier to work with people who are positive in their outlook, and we are much more likely to want to work with such people than with those who seem negative. If rural church members have a contribution to make to life in the countryside, that contribution will most likely be limited if they are not perceived in the wider community as being people with whom others would like to work. So the rural church needs to be careful that its members do not become so absorbed in keeping the church running that they lose sight of the deep joy that comes from a life of discipleship. If this entails letting certain aspects of church life diminish – a Sunday school that is barely attended, say, or an Evensong that only a handful of congregants come to, because they feel duty bound to support it – then this is to be encouraged. It is to be encouraged because it might provide a means by which the Church can actually flourish, by freeing its members for more fruitful service elsewhere (a point I made in Chapter 5 in relation to the involvement of church members in rural schools).

More fundamentally, I am suggesting that the rural church needs to recover a sense of the joy of discipleship. In this way, it can make a significant contribution to the communities of which it is a part, by showing that the theological story of community is one in which we come to life in all its fullness. If you need to be persuaded of the significance of joyfulness to rural theology, imagine acting on some of the suggestions I have offered in this book in a way that is characterized by exhaustion,

---

6 Thomson, John, 2010, *Living Holiness*, London: Epworth Press, p. 3.

feelings of resentment and perhaps even unfriendliness to one's neighbours – all of which can sometimes be in evidence among those of us who belong to the rural church. First, it is unlikely that anyone with such an outlook would even be motivated to act in the ways described. Second, even if we are, it seems hard to imagine that the people with whose lives ours intersect will feel as if they see anything of the risen Christ in us. And third, since the eucharistic practice of the Church is primarily focused on serving the world, we might say action that appears to do this grudgingly is not really eucharistic action at all.

So the rural church needs to be a place of joy. It needs to show the world around it that the Eucharist is an opportunity to give thanks and praise to God, to celebrate his gifts to us, and to share those gifts far and wide. It needs to show that the life of disciple-ship is a gift from God, rather than a cross to bear, and that com-ing into the risen Christ's presence is the biggest treat we can have. In this way, not only will the good will of faithful Christians sparkle like a jewel, but the rural church itself will sparkle, at-tracting new pilgrims and sharing Christ's love and justice with the communities of which its members are a part.

Children and the Eucharist

There are certain structural ways in which the rural church can share the joy of life in Christ among the communities in which it is set. In this section, I want to suggest that the rural church ought to consider admitting baptized people to the Eucharist even if they have not been confirmed; recognizing that doing so is part of its ministry of friendship and welcome in the lo-cal community. This is a particular issue in relation to ministry among children and young people, who might well feel excluded by church policies that require confirmation before participation in the Eucharist and who might well, as a result, decide not to continue attending church.[7] Given that children and young people are in a minority in our churches anyway, this seems like a good enough reason in itself to consider adjusting the rules for admittance to Holy Communion.

There is a bigger reason, though, which has to do with enabling people to come into the worshipping community of the Church and take their place in the drama of salvation history. If the Church excludes from the Eucharist churchgoers who are not confirmed, then it closes the possibility of these people coming fully into the life of the Church. In rural communities, where the Church has the potential to make a significant contribution to the flourishing of local communities, opening the Eucharist to a wider range of people seems like a sensible step for it to take. Indeed, it might be said that such a decision would itself be a sign that the Church is living its Eucharist for the good of the world.

The history of the rules governing admittance to the Eucharist is sketchy. St Augustine was an advocate of admitting children to the Eucharist, arguing that there can be 'no halfway house between the unbaptized and the communicant', such as the notion of confirmation seems to imply.[8] Augustine's view may well have been informed by the statement Jesus makes in the Fourth Gospel: 'Unless you eat the flesh of the Son of Man and drink his blood, you have no life in you' (John 6.53). This certainly seems to be an important text in understanding the significance of participation in the Eucharist to a life of discipleship. Even so, the western tradition of Christianity has been surprisingly ambivalent about admitting children and people who are not confirmed to the Eucharist. Even today, the Church of England's official position is that diocesan bishops must grant

---

7 Jackson, H., 2004, 'Children at the Font and Altar', *Church Times*, 26 November, p. 10.

8 Howells, Ann and Littler, Keith, 2007, 'Children and Communion: Listening to Churchwardens in Rural and Urban Wales', *Rural Theology*, vol. 5, part 1, p. 14.

permission for parishes to allow baptized children to take the bread and wine if they are not confirmed, and that baptized adults may only participate in the Eucharist if they have decided to seek confirmation.[9]

Ann Howells's and Keith Littler's research about the Church in Wales shows that clergy are far more open to the idea of children receiving Eucharist than the laity.[10] If a similar pattern is true across rural parishes in the rest of the UK, then it seems as if the clergy have a particular role in educating congregation members about the role of the Eucharist in Christian formation. If the Church is willing to share its Eucharist among members of the community, who have been initiated into the Church's worshipping life by virtue of their baptism, but who have not yet been confirmed, it shows a ministry of welcome and openness to the wider community. Many more people in rural communities would be able to participate in the Eucharist if confirmation were not necessary to such participation; it would enable the Church in the countryside to offer a confident welcome to rural residents, which might well reflect Christ's own practice in eating with people in order to get alongside them (for example, Luke 5.29; Mark 2.15; Luke 19.1 ff. – and so it goes).

Timothy Gorringe asserts that Christ's habit of eating with people is 'an instrument in his purpose of making people whole',[11] and we might well see the Eucharist in this light. Thus, through participation in the Eucharist, would-be pilgrims are given a chance to locate themselves in the narrative by which the Church is constituted; they are given a chance to be made whole, to become Christlike; they are shown what it means to live for the good of the other, as Christ lives for us.

---

9 http://www.cofe.anglican.org/lifeevents/baptismconfirm/sectionc. html (accessed March 2010).

10 Howells and Littler, 2007, 'Children and Communion', p. 18.

11 Gorringe, Timothy, 1997, *Sign of Love: Reflections on the Eucharist*, London: SPCK, p. 18.

Gorringe goes a step further than me, in asserting that Christ's table fellowship with people suggests an inversion of the expected order in which baptism precedes participation in the Eucharist.[12] This might seem an appealing approach for the rural church, if the arguments I am offering in favour of admitting children and people who have not been confirmed to the Eucharist are found to be persuasive. After all, by welcoming at the eucharistic table those who are not baptized, the Church shows a Christlike willingness to share its life with all comers. But baptism enables disciples to be initiated into the Christian community; to become oriented, if you will, to the narrative of salvation history. Without such orientation, I suggest the Eucharist loses its meaning, and that participation in it contributes nothing to formation as a disciple of Christ. The House of Bishops of the Church of England says of the Eucharist: 'It unites Creation and Redemption, life and liturgy, porch and altar. It galvanizes Christians for witness and service in the world and strengthens us to go forth for Christ to win others for his cause.'[13] This statement assumes that those who participate in the Eucharist have some fundamental orientation to the drama of salvation history, that they know what it means to image the trinitarian God and to eat Christ's body and drink his blood. Such orientation comes through baptism, where Christians are welcomed into the Church as those who might come to participate fully in its sacramental life. The rural church might well welcome children and people who have not been confirmed to participate in the Eucharist as part of a ministry of welcome and friendship to the rural communities in which it is located. But if such participants are to be transformed, it is my belief that they ought properly to be baptized into a life of faith in order that they may be full participants in the Eucharist.

---

12 Gorringe, *Sign of Love*, p. 24.

13 House of Bishops of the Church of England, 2001, *The Eucharist: Sacrament of Unity*, London: Church House Publishing, p. 5.

That is not to say that the rural church should not take Gorringe's observations concerning Jesus' table fellowship seriously, though. I have been arguing throughout the book that the rural church can be a Eucharist for the good of the world and that, in doing so, it can help to build community in the countryside. When the Church takes its eucharistic life seriously, its other practices are shot through with eucharistic values. That is, the wider activities of the Church are ones in which friendship and unselfishness are central, and in which an acceptance of human frailty can be taken for granted. Thus, in being a Eucharist for the rural communities it serves, the Church in the countryside opens its everyday life – its non-sacramental practices, if you like – to the wider community. This might involve eating and drinking with other members of the local community on a regular basis, or organizing parties that celebrate and give thanks for God's gifts in creation. Harvest suppers are a fine opportunity for this, but really no excuse is needed.

If the rural church is joyful in its engagement with the wider community, and its members seek to engage with other rural dwellers as often as they can in ways that are Christlike, then the Church will discover that more and more people show an interest in participating in its sacramental life, as well. And if such people are welcomed to the eucharistic table as soon as possible (that is, once they are baptized, with no need for confirmation), then they can begin to be transformed by Christ's saving work, and take their place in the drama of salvation history by imaging the trinitarian God.

Extended Communion

Extended Communion is the practice of using eucharistic elements that have been consecrated by a priest in a service that is led at a later time, and perhaps in a different location, by a licensed lay person or deacon. There is not much to say about it, other than to assert that, given what I have been arguing about the centrality of the Eucharist to the worshipping life of the rural church, it is a practice for which I believe provision should be made where necessary. In *Faith in the Countryside* the Archbishops' Commission recognized that, for many churches, extended Communion represents the only means of church members receiving frequent Holy Communion. The report urged that the House of Bishops review its discussions about the practice, with a particular concern for rural parishes in which priests are in short supply.[14] This recommendation has since been taken up, and the current rules in the Church of England stipulate that, as with admitting children to the Eucharist, extended Communion is allowed with the permission of the diocesan bishop. Other denominations are less circumspect about the practice, and the short-staffed Roman Catholic Church in particular relies on it as a means of safeguarding its sacramental life.

It is my belief that the rural church should embrace the opportunity provided by extended Communion to engage in regular eucharistic worship, in which its members encounter the risen Christ through the breaking of bread and the sharing of wine. Rural clergy frequently have responsibility for clusters of churches, and it is unreasonable to expect that they can be present in each one of them every week in order to celebrate the Eucharist. But where extended Communion is an option, rural congregations will still be able to participate in weekly Eucharists, and thereby be formed to share Christ's love and justice with the world.

The objection to extended Communion, as *Faith in the Countryside* notes, is that Christ is present in the sacrament, but is not 'welded' to the bread and wine.[15] To put it another way, we come

---

14 ACORA, 1990, *Faith in the Countryside*, Worthing: Churchman Publishing, p. 190.

15 ACORA, *Faith in the Countryside*, p. 190.

into the risen Christ's presence in a particular eucharistic act, at a particular time and in a particular place. Taking bread and wine that are consecrated in one act of worship and distributing them among a different worshipping community may seem to be problematic, because it ignores the theological understanding of how Christ is present in the sacraments. But the practice of reserved sacrament nullifies this objection, since it assumes it is possible to set consecrated elements aside and share them among worshippers – in this case the sick or dying – on a different occasion, and in a different place if need be. Reserving the sacrament involves implicit recognition that imbibing the eucharistic elements is important in itself to being transformed by the risen Christ, even if they have by necessity been consecrated elsewhere. I want to argue that a similar understanding of the Eucharist undergirds a defence of Communion by extension in rural churches.

As with the discussion of admitting children and people who have not been confirmed to the Eucharist, my analysis of extended Communion resides in recognition of the power of the Eucharist to transform Christian disciples so that they become Christlike. A theme that has dominated this book is the centrality of the Eucharist to the rural church's interaction with the wider rural community: in an era of dwindling church attendance and decreased vocations, we need to think seriously about the ways in which we can safeguard regular celebration of the Eucharist in our rural churches. The two ways of doing this that I have considered in this chapter possess the twin merits of being pragmatic and thoroughly theological. The church in the countryside does well to embrace them.

Concluding remarks

By loosening restrictions on participation in, and celebration of, the Eucharist and being a joyful presence in the communities in which it is located, the Church in the countryside can help those communities to flourish. This is because the Eucharist is a practice that builds community, by enabling disciples to take their place in the drama of salvation history and image the trinitarian God. It is through the Eucharist that rural theology finds its clearest expression; the Eucharist embodies the theological story I have been telling about community in this book, and it forms disciples to share Christ's love and justice far and wide. Through participation in the Eucharist we are shown how to be friends, trained out of selfish ways and reminded that God loves us because of our frailty. More significantly, we are reminded that, as those who belong to the new creation, we must be in right relationship with the rest of creation, and with one another.

Thus, in the Eucharist, the Church gives expression to the idea that has been central to this book: namely, that community is intrinsically good, to be desired for its own sake rather than for the benefits that derive from participating in it. In imaging the trinitarian God, we are called to be other-facing, and this means that our primary concern is for the good of the other. The Eucharist trains us out of self-interest, and demonstrates why those accounts of community that reduce it to a social contract (such as the theory of justice associated with John Rawls, which I considered in Chapter 1) or social capital (which I discussed in Chapter 3) are impoverished and incomplete. Being human consists in caring about our fellow creatures in ways that are Christlike, and thereby inherently other-regarding. As we are engaged with the rural communities in which we live, those of us who are formed through participation in the Eucharist seek to live our theological story about community in ways that transform the world in which we are called to love and serve the Lord – who lived, died, was raised and ascended for the sake of the new creation.

This book represents an attempt to unpack some of the theological assumptions that might be taken to undergird the interaction of the Church in the countryside with wider rural communities. As I said at the start, it can be surprising to see that much of what we assume to be common sense is grounded in our participation in the practice of the Eucharist, and is therefore thoroughly theological. Much has changed in the countryside in the 20 years since *Faith in the Countryside* was published. But the Church's call to embody a story about community that speaks of the proper relation of humans to the non-human world, and to one another, remains.

Rural theology is the activity of giving expression to the theological story about community in ways that give life to rural churches and to rural communities, as well as giving hope to Christian disciples who live in the countryside and are formed through participation in the worshipping life of the rural church. There is, as I suggested in Chapter 2, a strong sense of community in rural areas, and a hankering after it among many rural residents. The Church in the countryside, because it has the best story to tell concerning what it means to live in community with one's fellow creatures, therefore has a distinctive role to play in rural life. Regular participation in the Eucharist will enable the rural church's members to better fulfil that role, by forming them and helping them to build communities that flourish. But if what we do inside church forms us, it is what we do beyond it that really matters. So, as we are dismissed from our sharing of bread and wine, as we go out of the sacramental presence of the risen Lord to love and serve him in the rural context, it is at this moment that rural theology locates itself. Or, to put it another way, it is at the moment of sending that our work as disciples really begins.

A Note on Sources

All of the literature referred to in this text can be traced by means of the footnotes. For this reason, I have decided against including a full bibliography, but instead, offer a short list of recommended reading for anyone who is interested in doing more work in rural theology.

Rural theology and the care of creation

Archbishops' Commission on Rural Areas (ACORA), 1990, *Faith in the Countryside*, Worthing: Churchman Publishing.

Arthur Rank Centre, 2000, *Celebrating the Rural Church: 10 Years on from Faith in the Countryside*, Stoneleigh: ACORA Publishing.

Gaze, Sally, 2007, *Mission-Shaped and Rural: Growing Churches in the Countryside*, London: Church House Publishing.

Gorringe, Timothy, 2006, *Harvest: Food, Farming and the Churches*, London: SPCK.

Martineau, Jeremy, Francis, Leslie and Francis, Peter (eds), 2004, *Changing Rural Life*, Norwich: Canterbury Press.

Smith, Alan, 2008, *God-Shaped Mission: Theological and Practical Perspectives on the Rural Church*, Norwich: Canterbury Press.

Southgate, Christopher, 2008, *The Groaning of Creation*, Louisville: Westminster John Knox Press.

Rural life in literary perspective

Blythe, Ronald, 2005, *Akenfield*, London: Penguin Classics.

Taylor, Craig, 2006, *Return to Akenfield*, London: Granta Books.

The Eucharist and Christian life

Gorringe, Timothy, 1997, *The Sign of Love: Reflections on the Eucharist*, London: SPCK.

Hauerwas, Stanley and Wells, Samuel (eds), 2006, *The Blackwell Companion to Christian Ethics*, Oxford: Blackwell.

Radcliffe, Timothy, 2008, *Why Go to Church?*, London: Continuum.

Wells, Samuel, 2006, *God's Companions: Reimagining Christian Ethics*, Oxford: Blackwell Publishing.

Web resources

www.ruralcommunities.gov.uk – the website of the Commission for Rural Communities.

www.rural-theology.org.uk – the website of the Rural Theology Association.

www.arthurrankcentre.org.uk – the website of the Arthur Rank Centre, Stoneleigh, Warwickshire.

Index of Subjects

Index of Names